W9-DCH-498

21926

THE ENCYCLOPEDIA OF PSYCHOACTIVE DRUGS

SERIES 1

The Addictive Personality
Alcohol and Alcoholism
Alcohol Customs and Rituals
Alcohol Teenage Drinking
Amphetamines Danger in the Fast Lane
Barbiturates Sleeping Potion or Intoxicant?
Caffeine The Most Popular Stimulant
Cocaine A New Epidemic
Escape from Anxiety and Stress
Flowering Plants Magic in Bloom
Getting Help Treatments for Drug Abuse
Heroin The Street Narcotic
Inhalants The Toxic Fumes

LSD Visions or Nightmares?
Marijuana Its Effects on Mind & Body
Methadone Treatment for Addiction
Mushrooms Psychedelic Fungi
Nicotine An Old-Fashioned Addiction
Over-The-Counter Drugs Harmless or Hazardous?
PCP The Dangerous Angel
Prescription Narcotics The Addictive Painkillers
Quaaludes The Quest for Oblivion
Teenage Depression and Drugs
Treating Mental Illness
Valium and Other Tranquilizers

SERIES 2

Bad Trips
Brain Function
Case Histories
Celebrity Drug Use
Designer Drugs
The Downside of Drugs
Drinking, Driving, and Drugs
Drugs and Civilization
Drugs and Crime
Drugs and Diet
Drugs and Disease
Drugs and Emotion
Drugs and Pain
Drugs and Perception
Drugs and Pregnancy
Drugs and Sexual Behavior

Drugs and Sleep
Drugs and Sports
Drugs and the Arts
Drugs and the Brain
Drugs and the Family
Drugs and the Law
Drugs and Women
Drugs of the Future
Drugs Through the Ages
Drug Use Around the World
Legalization: A Debate
Mental Disturbances
Nutrition and the Brain
The Origins and Sources of Drugs
Substance Abuse: Prevention and Treatment
Who Uses Drugs?

DESIGNER DRUGS

GENERAL EDITOR
Professor Solomon H. Snyder, M.D.

*Distinguished Service Professor of
Neuroscience, Pharmacology, and Psychiatry at
The Johns Hopkins University School of Medicine*

•

ASSOCIATE EDITOR
Professor Barry L. Jacobs, Ph.D.

*Program in Neuroscience, Department of Psychology,
Princeton University*

•

SENIOR EDITORIAL CONSULTANT
Joann Rodgers

*Deputy Director, Office of Public Affairs at
The Johns Hopkins Medical Institutions*

THE ENCYCLOPEDIA OF PSYCHOACTIVE DRUGS
SERIES 2
DESIGNER DRUGS

PAULA GOODMAN & GABRIEL KOZ, M.D.

CHELSEA HOUSE PUBLISHERS
NEW YORK • PHILADELPHIA

EDITOR-IN-CHIEF: Nancy Toff
EXECUTIVE EDITOR: Remmel T. Nunn
MANAGING EDITOR: Karyn Gullen Browne
COPY CHIEF: Juliann Barbato
PICTURE EDITOR: Adrian G. Allen
ART DIRECTOR: Giannella Garrett
MANUFACTURING MANAGER: Gerald Levine

Staff for DESIGNER DRUGS:

SENIOR EDITOR: Jane Larkin Crain
ASSOCIATE EDITOR: Paula Edelson
ASSISTANT EDITOR: Laura-Ann Dolce
COPY EDITORS: Karen Hammonds, James Guiry
EDITORIAL ASSISTANT: Susan DeRosa
ASSOCIATE PICTURE EDITOR: Juliette Dickstein
PICTURE RESEARCHER: Debra Hershkowitz
DESIGNER: Victoria Tomaselli
DESIGN ASSISTANT: Donna Sinisgalli
PRODUCTION COORDINATOR: Joseph Romano
COVER ILLUSTRATION: Linda Draper

CREATIVE DIRECTOR: Harold Steinberg

3 5 7 9 8 6 4 2

Library of Congress Cataloging in Publication Data

Goodman, Paula.
  Designer Drugs.
  (The Encyclopedia of psychoactive drugs. Series 2)
  Bibliography: p.
  Includes index.
  1. Designer drugs—Juvenile literature. 2. Drug abuse—Juvenile literature.
I. Gabriel Koz, M.D.   II. Title.   III. Series.
RM316.G66   1987   362.2'93   87-26835
ISBN 1-55546-207-3
    0-7910-0781-2 (pbk.)

CONTENTS

A pharmacist dispenses prescription medication. Designer drugs are often inept copies of legitimate drugs; the effects of these amateur concoctions are dangerous and potentially lethal.

FOREWORD

In the Mainstream
of American Life

One of the legacies of the social upheaval of the 1960s is that psychoactive drugs have become part of the mainstream of American life. Schools, homes, and communities cannot be "drug proofed." There is a demand for drugs — and the supply is plentiful. Social norms have changed and drugs are not only available—they are everywhere.

But where efforts to curtail the supply of drugs and outlaw their use have had tragically limited effects on demand, it may be that education has begun to stem the rising tide of drug abuse among young people and adults alike.

Over the past 25 years, as drugs have become an increasingly routine facet of contemporary life, a great many teenagers have adopted the notion that drug taking was somehow a right or a privilege or a necessity. They have done so, however, without understanding the consequences of drug use during the crucial years of adolescence.

The teenage years are few in the total life cycle, but critical in the maturation process. During these years adolescents face the difficult tasks of discovering their identity, clarifying their sexual roles, asserting their independence, learning to cope with authority, and searching for goals that will give their lives meaning.

Drugs rob adolescents of precious time, stamina, and health. They interrupt critical learning processes, sometimes forever. Teenagers who use drugs are likely to withdraw increasingly into themselves, to "cop out" at just the time when they most need to reach out and experience the world.

Graffiti on a ghetto wall announces that New York City is "crack city." Crack is a designer version of cocaine, and has proven to be the most addictive of all illicit drugs to hit the streets.

Fortunately, as a recent Gallup poll shows, young people are beginning to realize this, too. They themselves label drugs their most important problem. In the last few years, moreover, the climate of tolerance and ignorance surrounding drugs has been changing.

Adolescents as well as adults are becoming aware of mounting evidence that every race, ethnic group, and class is vulnerable to drug dependency.

Recent publicity about the cost and failure of drug rehabilitation efforts; dangerous drug use among pilots, air traffic controllers, star athletes, and Hollywood celebrities; and drug-related accidents, suicides, and violent crime have focused the public's attention on the need to wage an all-out war on drug abuse before it seriously undermines the fabric of society itself.

The anti-drug message is getting stronger and there is evidence that the message is beginning to get through to adults and teenagers alike.

The Encyclopedia of Psychoactive Drugs hopes to play a part in the national campaign now underway to educate young people about drugs. Series 1 provides clear and comprehensive discussions of common psychoactive substances, outlines their psychological and physiological effects on the mind and body, explains how they "hook" the user, and separates fact from myth in the complex issue of drug abuse.

Whereas Series 1 focuses on specific drugs, such as nicotine or cocaine, Series 2 confronts a broad range of both social and physiological phenomena. Each volume addresses the ramifications of drug use and abuse on some aspect of human experience: social, familial, cultural, historical, and physical. Separate volumes explore questions about the effects of drugs on brain chemistry and unborn children; the use and abuse of painkillers; the relationship between drugs and sexual behavior, sports, and the arts; drugs and disease; the role of drugs in history; and the sophisticated drugs now being developed in the laboratory that will profoundly change the future.

Each book in the series is fully illustrated and is tailored to the needs and interests of young readers. The more adolescents know about drugs and their role in society, the less likely they are to misuse them.

Joann Rodgers
Senior Editorial Consultant

Pandora unleashes all the ills that plague the human race. Designer drugs could proliferate like another of Pandora's woes unless the public is made aware of the threat they constitute.

INTRODUCTION

The Gift of Wizardry
Use and Abuse

JACK H. MENDELSON, M.D.
NANCY K. MELLO, Ph.D.
Alcohol and Drug Abuse Research Center
Harvard Medical School—McLean Hospital

Dorothy to the Wizard:

"I think you are a very bad man," said Dorothy.
"Oh no, my dear; I'm really a very good man; but I'm a very bad Wizard."
—from THE WIZARD OF OZ

Man is endowed with the gift of wizardry, a talent for discovery and invention. The discovery and invention of substances that change the way we feel and behave are among man's special accomplishments, and, like so many other products of our wizardry, these substances have the capacity to harm as well as to help. Psychoactive drugs can cause profound changes in the chemistry of the brain and other vital organs, and although their legitimate use can relieve pain and cure disease, their abuse leads in a tragic number of cases to destruction.

Consider alcohol — available to all and yet regarded with intense ambivalence from biblical times to the present day. The use of alcoholic beverages dates back to our earliest ancestors. Alcohol use and misuse became associated with the worship of gods and demons. One of the most powerful Greek gods was Dionysus, lord of fruitfulness and god of wine. The Romans adopted Dionysus but changed his name to Bacchus. Festivals and holidays associated with Bacchus celebrated the harvest and the origins of life. Time has blurred the images of the Bacchanalian festival, but the theme of

13

drunkenness as a major part of celebration has survived the pagan gods and remains a familiar part of modern society. The term "Bacchanalian Festival" conveys a more appealing image than "drunken orgy" or "pot party," but whatever the label, drinking alcohol is a form of drug use that results in addiction for millions.

The fact that many millions of other people can use alcohol in moderation does not mitigate the toll this drug takes on society as a whole. According to reliable estimates, one out of every ten Americans develops a serious alcohol-related problem sometime in his or her lifetime. In addition, automobile accidents caused by drunken drivers claim the lives of tens of thousands every year. Many of the victims are gifted young people, just starting out in adult life. Hospital emergency rooms abound with patients seeking help for alcohol-related injuries.

Who is to blame? Can we blame the many manufacturers who produce such an amazing variety of alcoholic beverages? Should we blame the educators who fail to explain the perils of intoxication, or so exaggerate the dangers of drinking that no one could possibly believe them? Are friends to blame — those peers who urge others to "drink more and faster," or the macho types who stress the importance of being able to "hold your liquor"? Casting blame, however, is hardly constructive, and pointing the finger is a fruitless way to deal with the problem. Alcoholism and drug abuse have few culprits but many victims. Accountability begins with each of us, every time we choose to use or misuse an intoxicating substance.

It is ironic that some of man's earliest medicines, derived from natural plant products, are used today to poison and to intoxicate. Relief from pain and suffering is one of society's many continuing goals. Over 3,000 years ago, the Therapeutic Papyrus of Thebes, one of our earliest written records, gave instructions for the use of opium in the treatment of pain. Opium, in the form of its major derivative, morphine, and similar compounds, such as heroin, have also been used by many to induce changes in mood and feeling. Another example of man's misuse of a natural substance is the coca leaf, which for centuries was used by the Indians of Peru to reduce fatigue and hunger. Its modern derivative, cocaine, has important medical use as a local anesthetic. Unfortunately, its increasing abuse in the 1980s clearly has reached epidemic proportions.

The purpose of this series is to explore in depth the psychological and behavioral effects that psychoactive drugs have on the individual, and also, to investigate the ways in which drug use influences the legal, economic, cultural, and even moral aspects of societies. The information presented here (and in other books in this series) is based on many clinical and laboratory studies and other observations by people from diverse walks of life.

Over the centuries, novelists, poets, and dramatists have provided us with many insights into the sometimes seductive but ultimately problematic aspects of alcohol and drug use. Physicians, lawyers, biologists, psychologists, and social scientists have contributed to a better understanding of the causes and consequences of using these substances. The authors in this series have attempted to gather and condense all the latest information about drug use and abuse. They have also described the sometimes wide gaps in our knowledge and have suggested some new ways to answer many difficult questions.

One such question, for example, is how do alcohol and drug problems get started? And what is the best way to treat them when they do? Not too many years ago, alcoholics and drug abusers were regarded as evil, immoral, or both. It is now recognized that these persons suffer from very complicated diseases involving deep psychological and social problems. To understand how the disease begins and progresses, it is necessary to understand the nature of the substance, the behavior of addicts, and the characteristics of the society or culture in which they live.

Although many of the social environments we live in are very similar, some of the most subtle differences can strongly influence our thinking and behavior. Where we live, go to school and work, whom we discuss things with — all influence our opinions about drug use and misuse. Yet we also share certain commonly accepted beliefs that outweigh any differences in our attitudes. The authors in this series have tried to identify and discuss the central, most crucial issues concerning drug use and misuse.

Despite the increasing sophistication of the chemical substances we create in the laboratory, we have a long way to go in our efforts to make these powerful drugs work for us rather than against us.

The volumes in this series address a wide range of timely questions. What influence has drug use had on the arts? Why do so many of today's celebrities and star athletes use drugs, and what is being done to solve this problem? What is the relationship between drugs and crime? What is the physiological basis for the power drugs can hold over us? These are but a few of the issues explored in this far-ranging series.

Educating people about the dangers of drugs can go a long way towards minimizing the desperate consequences of substance abuse for individuals and society as a whole. Luckily, human beings have the resources to solve even the most serious problems that beset them, once they make the commitment to do so. As one keen and sensitive observer, Dr. Lewis Thomas, has said,

> There is nothing at all absurd about the human condition. We matter. It seems to me a good guess, hazarded by a good many people who have thought about it, that we may be engaged in the formation of something like a mind for the life of this planet. If this is so, we are still at the most primitive stage, still fumbling with language and thinking, but infinitely capacitated for the future. Looked at this way, it is remarkable that we've come as far as we have in so short a period, really no time at all as geologists measure time. We are the newest, youngest, and the brightest thing around.

DESIGNER DRUGS

Crack and crack vials. This concentrated form of cocaine is a central nervous system stimulant that can cause stroke and heart failure.

CHAPTER 1

WHAT ARE DESIGNER DRUGS?

They're called designer drugs because the jet-set uses them. They're glamorous drugs—like cocaine."

"They're drugs that cost a lot, like designer jeans."

"They're called designer drugs because they can be designed to act like any drug you want."

"Aren't they prescription drugs?"

"Hallucinogens. . . ."

These are actual responses to the question, "What do *you* think designer drugs are?" They are, for the most part, incorrect.

Hallucinogens, for example, are not the only forms of designer drugs. Nor are designer drugs necessarily expensive. In some cases, they may even cost less than the drugs they replace on the black market.

It is true that designer drugs are indirectly related to prescription drugs, and there is a grain of truth in the idea that chemists "design . . . any drug you want." But few people truly understand what is meant by the term "designer drug," or the dangers in using one.

Dr. Gary Henderson, a pharmacologist working at the University of California, first used the term "designer drugs" in the early 1980s to describe *synthetic* or lab-produced analogs of prescription drugs controlled by the U.S. Food and Drug Administration (FDA).

Researcher Dr. Gary Henderson of the University of California at Davis discusses the chemical makeup of methyl-fentanyl, a designer opiate.

An *analog* is a compound whose chemical structure closely resembles the structure of its parent drug. Analogs may also be called *derivatives*, to indicate that they are chemically derived from a parent drug.

The chemical structure of a designer drug may differ from the structure of its parent drug by only a few atoms. But until late 1986 the laws regulating drug research and production in the United States allowed for the legal production and sale of these chemical analogs of illegal or controlled drugs. As long as the designer imitations were only similar, but not identical to, controlled drugs, underground chemists could not be prosecuted or fined for making them.

The term "designer drug" can also refer to a known, abused drug that has been repackaged or redesigned for easier use or increased appeal to consumers. "Crack" is a designer form of cocaine. Because it is "ready-to-smoke" it may appeal to users unwilling to snort it, unable to inject it, or frightened to heat or "freebase it" in order to use it. (Comedian Richard Pryor was heating cocaine when he accidentally set himself on fire in 1980 and nearly lost his life.)

Designer Drug Groups

Designer *opiates* include 1-methyl-4-phenyl-4-proprionoxy-piperidine (MPPP) and the fentanyl derivatives. As many as a dozen derivatives have been detected in drug samples, but the most-publicized of these are alpha-methyl-fentanyl and 3-methyl-fentanyl.

Designer *hallucinogens* include methylenedioxyme-thamphetamine (MDMA, "Ecstasy") and derivatives of phencyclidine (PCP or "angel dust").

Designer *stimulants* include "crack," a purified form of cocaine.

Drugs in each of these groups affect the central nervous system (the brain and spinal cord) in various ways. Consequently, the "highs," body-wide effects, and dangers of overdose are different for each of these drugs.

Designer *opiates* duplicate the effects of pharmaceutical drugs of the opiate class, such as heroin and morphine. In a medical setting, *opiates* such as morphine provide *analgesia* (pain relief) and *anesthesia* (partial or complete loss of sensation). Very generally stated, opiates slow or reduce functions of the nervous system. They slow down the heart rate,

Molecular drawings of meperidine, a narcotic, and MPPP, the "copy cat" drug modeled after it, illustrate the structural similarities between the two compounds. Both produce euphoria and rapid addiction.

breathing rate, and rate of digestion. They constrict the pupils of the eyes. Relatively small overdoses of these drugs can cause death.

Overdose deaths from designer opiates are the result of a bodywide "slowdown" taken to its logical conclusion — a "full stop"—coma, convulsions, or *cardiorespiratory arrest*.

Designer *stimulants* (analogs of amphetamines and cocaine) *increase* the total amount of central nervous system activity. They increase the blood pressure, heart rate, and bodywide restlessness and arousal. They also dilate the pupils of the eyes.

Overdose death from *central nervous system (CNS) stimulants* can be described figuratively as death from a "blow-up" or "explosion," in which the body's vital functions are driven beyond the limits of their capacity and endurance, whether in the form of a heart attack combined with increased blood pressure, a *stroke* (rupture of blood vessels in the brain), or in some other way.

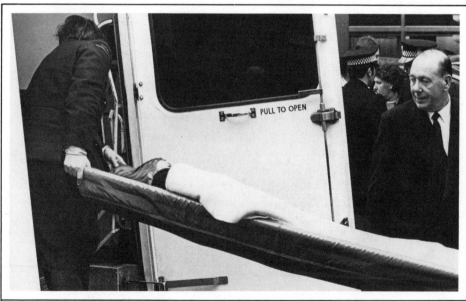

An overdose victim is lifted into an ambulance. All opiates have a high overdose potential. This is especially true of designer narcotics, because it is impossible to predict their potency.

Designer *hallucinogens* (analogs of LSD, MDA, or PCP) act primarily to distort perception and thought, so that under the influence of these drugs users are in a temporary state of drug-induced psychosis, or mentally out of contact with reality. In addition, designer hallucinogens may reproduce some of the effects of CNS stimulants, including restlessness, an increased heart and breathing rate, and, to a lesser degree, dilation of the pupils of the eyes.

The Question of Legality

The U.S. Food and Drug Administration classifies drugs under five *schedules*, according to their medical usefulness in relation to their potential for abuse.

Schedule I includes drugs with a high potential for abuse, and no current legal medical use in this country. Examples of Schedule I drugs are heroin, LSD, and marijuana. To manufacture these drugs, companies, individuals, and universities need a research license. Large fines, jail terms, or both are used to penalize the unauthorized manufacture, sale, or possession of Schedule I drugs.

Schedule II drugs are *prescription* drugs with a high to moderate abuse potential but with recognized medical usefulness. Meperidine and fentanyl are Schedule II drugs, as are cocaine and some of the amphetamines. Cocaine remains a useful local anesthetic. Amphetamines can be used to treat the condition known as narcolepsy, in which sleeping spells may occur suddenly at any hour of the day.

Schedules III and IV include drugs with less abuse potential and fewer restrictions on their sale. Schedule V drugs include many "over-the-counter" (non-prescription) drugs.

Until late 1986, the FDA was permitted to outlaw individual drugs on a "case-by-case" basis, but not permitted to outlaw entire groups of drugs. Because of this policy, designer drugs, being chemically similar to Schedule I and II drugs, but not actually identical to them, fell outside the power of the FDA.

The limits to the FDA's power may have been intended to encourage drug companies and researchers to explore the actions of all the members of a particular family or group of drugs.

Pharmaceutical corporations routinely test promising drugs by synthesizing a series of such chemically related compounds or analogs. Such a series may contain several dozen compounds that researchers manipulate in several different ways. For example, the central molecule or chemical "core" of the parent or original drug in the series may be retained, but the side branches or chains of atoms attached to this core may be changed, substituted, or repositioned in the lab.

Scientists manipulate the chemical structure to be sure they have not overlooked a truly new and useful drug member in a series, or to see whether they can retain the medical action of a drug but reduce its unpleasant or unwanted "side" effects. Often, they will attempt to imitate a drug patented by another company without getting sued by that company for violating its patent on the drug.

Underground chemists also synthesize a number of related compounds in a series, the parent drug of which belongs to one of the FDA's regulated schedules. In this way, they exploit a sophisticated, legitimate research technique for illicit ends.

The Crucial Differences

Science writer Roger Highfield wrote in his article "Designer Drugs," which appeared in *World Health* in 1986, that "Drug companies aim to make products with enhanced activity and few side effects.... By contrast, the underground chemists are trying to make a legal version of an illegal substance, with little concern for drug trials, quality control, or side effects."

Pharmaceutical companies are required by law to test all drugs for safety and effectiveness before they can receive FDA approval to market them for medical use. Drugs must be tested on two species of mammals before tests on human volunteers are permitted. Animal tests are used to establish the right dose of the drug per unit of body weight, and the *LD50* — the lethal dose for 50% of the animals taking the drug.

Animal and clinical tests are unheard of in underground drug production. The test population is the population that buys the drug for illicit use. That is, the consumer is the lab rat of the underground chemist.

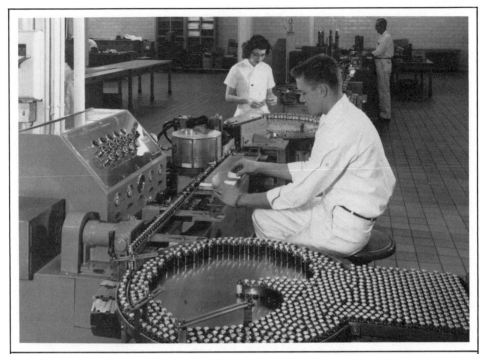

Pharmaceuticals move automatically through a labeling machine at a drug-manufacturing plant. The purity of drugs synthesized under such conditions is guaranteed through stringent quality controls.

If you stop to think about it, the *uniformity* of the dose, appearance, and action of most of the legitimate drugs we use is a small technological miracle. The amount of drug per capsule, tablet, or injection is machine-and-computer determined. Any inactive "filler" material added to an active drug to make a tablet, capsule, or solution must meet FDA standards for purity and uniformity. Similarly, the material used to enclose the drug (usually some form of gelatin) must be uniform in quality. Pharmaceuticals are stamped or otherwise coded with the manufacturer's logo, the dosage in which they are to be used, or both.

By contrast, irregularities in the amount of drug in a tablet or other dosage form, contamination, and adulteration of illicit drugs by other substances are the commonplaces of underground drug production, and have been for many years.

Package Labeling and Full Disclosure

If the FDA approves a drug for production on the basis of animal and clinical test results, the producer must also obey other regulations intended to publicize the uses of the drug as clearly as possible. For example, all drug samples sent to doctors or advertised to them must include a printed *Full Disclosure* statement. This statement gives a description of the drug, its actions, indications (what medical conditions it should be used to treat), contraindications (when and for whom it should not be used), warnings, adverse reactions (a list of all side effects), administration information (a description of how often and in what dosages the drug may be given), and clear listings of the dosages in which the drug is available.

Recently, there was a drug disaster involving a designer opiate with MPPP in California, in which several young people ingested a contaminated version of this designer drug. They suffered apparently irreversible brain damage, and today have been left with many of the symptoms of Parkinson's

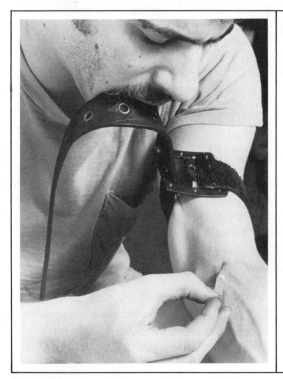

A man injects himself with heroin. All drugs obtained on the streets are cut with additives ranging from sugar to strychnine.

disease, a condition marked by involuntary tremors of the hands and other parts of the body. (This episode will be discussed further in chapter 5.) M. M. Kirsch, author of several articles on designer drugs, has pointed out that in the wake of this MPPP calamity, some black-market "recipes" for MPPP attached printed warnings that the drug, if incorrectly synthesized, could cause parkinsonism. Furthermore, underground manufacturers of MDMA ("Ecstasy") apparently printed circulars with instructions about the best setting in which to take the drug. These instances suggest that there is some self-regulation by designer drug manufacturers, but that it remains on a primitive level.

On the other hand, pharmaceutical companies undertake exhaustive testing of and publicity about their drugs' actions as required under federal law, and are penalized for noncompliance. They are accountable. Designer-drug chemists (and others in the drug "pipeline") are not accountable to federal agencies or to the consumers of the drugs they make. If they are employed by organized crime, they may be accountable to their employer. But the care with which they produce their drugs will always be a matter of personal, extralegal ethics.

The Drug Pipeline

Because designer drugs are synthetic chemicals rather than organic materials such as marijuana, coca leaves, or psychedelic mushrooms, designer drug production begins with the chemist and his employers, if any. The chemist needs a chemical recipe for the drug he will make, as well as lab equipment and the chemicals needed to make it.

Once the active agent is prepared, someone (not necessarily the chemist) must "cut" (mix with filler substances) and package the drug. Materials, such as lactose or milk sugar, that are used to cut drugs can be purchased in bulk from chemical houses or even health-food stores. Envelopes, plastic bags, and vials can be purchased in any number of places.

Once packaged, drug doses are transported to distributors or dealers. Designer drugs, because they are produced in the United States itself, are easier to transport than drugs produced abroad. There are no customs checks and no borders to cross.

An illegal drug sale on the streets of New York City. Despite law enforcement efforts to curb such blatant crimes, the sale of illicit substances goes unchecked in many cities throughout the world.

Distribution is perhaps the most publicized area of illicit drug production, simply because this is the point in the "pipe-line" at which the entire drug-making and selling operation "surfaces" in the person of the dealer. The dealer is the easiest person to identify and the most vulnerable person in the drug pipeline. He sells either in the street or in areas where several potential targets (consumers) can be contacted. Schools, clubs, and offices are examples of contact points, but any place where people regularly gather is a possible target area.

Finally, the consumer must find a way to ingest the drug. The highly profitable "head shops" full of drug paraphernalia that have cropped up over the past few years are one of the spin-offs of the underground drug industry.

As designer drugs move through the pipeline from the chemist to the packager, and then to the transporter and the dealer, there is always the possibility that something can go wrong, leaving the consumer to contend with the conse-quences.

For example, what if the chemist makes a mistake while preparing the drug? He can produce a totally unexpected substance, with different effects than he originally intended.

Or what if the material used to cut the drug is contaminated with other substances? Dust, talcum powder, even strychnine — a deadly poison — have all been found in drug samples. Or the amount of material used to cut the drug may be too small, producing a dose that is too strong. Or the active drug and the material used to cut it may not be mixed carefully enough.

These are probably the main dangers in the drug pipeline, but other possibilities abound. The transporter or the dealer could substitute one set of packages for another. Or they could misrepresent one drug as another.

Two points to keep in mind about the drug pipeline are: (1) the more middlemen separating the chemist from the drug user, the greater the risk of substitution, misrepresentation, and simple error; and (2) the more steps separating the chemist from the drug user, the smaller the chemist's sense of responsibility to the user.

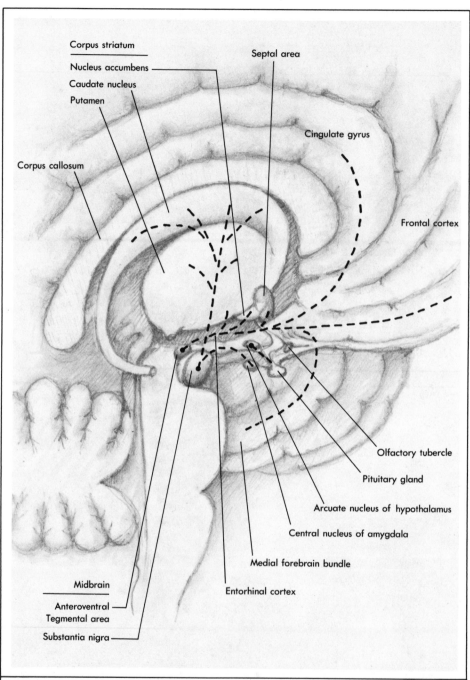

Corpus striatum
Nucleus accumbens
Caudate nucleus
Putamen

Septal area

Cingulate gyrus

Corpus callosum

Frontal cortex

Olfactory tubercle

Pituitary gland

Arcuate nucleus of hypothalamus

Central nucleus of amygdala

Medial forebrain bundle

Midbrain
Anteroventral
Tegmental area
Substantia nigra

Entorhinal cortex

Dopamine pathways in the brain. Researchers hope to discover the ways synthetic drugs influence neurochemistry by studying the ways in which dopamine and other neurotransmitters operate.

CHAPTER 2

THE BODY'S OWN DRUGS

We usually think of drugs as substances outside us that affect us if we smoke, swallow, or inject them. These drugs are *exogenous* (made outside the body) chemicals. But some substances made by the body can also be thought of as drugs. These *endogenous* (made inside the body) drugs are potent, richly varied in effect, completely pure, and free of damaging side effects. Without these drugs, which shape and balance every moment of our lives, we could not function. In this sense, all humans are "heavy drug users."

Two groups of endogenous drugs are especially important to brain and body function. They help the nerves in the brain communicate with the rest of the body by sending the chemical messages that shape our moods, thoughts, and behavior. We call these drugs *neurotransmitters* (transporters of nerve messages) and *neuromodulators* (regulators of nerve messages). Their discovery in the 20th century revolutionized the way we think of the body.

Acetylcholine was the first neurotransmitter to be discovered, in 1921. Since that time, several other chemicals that transmit nerve messages in the brain and remainder of the nervous system have been identified. These include *dopamine, norepinephrine, serotonin*, and *gamma-amino-butyric acid (GABA)*.

Most neurotransmitters serve multiple functions. Dopamine and norepinephrine are involved in the actions of stimulant drugs such as amphetamines and cocaine, and so presumably cause alertness under normal circumstances. Serotonin plays a role in sleep mechanisms. GABA is the major inhibitory neurotransmitter in the brain, and is involved in the effects of sedative drugs like barbiturates and antianxiety drugs such as Valium (diazepam).

Nerve cells in the brain synthesize and store these biochemicals so that they will be ready for use at all times. In fact, the ends of nerve cells, where they encounter other nerve cells along the path to an organ or tissue, have developed special, minute depots called *storage sites*, which contain chemicals such as neurotransmitters that can be released and reabsorbed after they have carried a signal or "message" from one nerve cell to its neighbor.

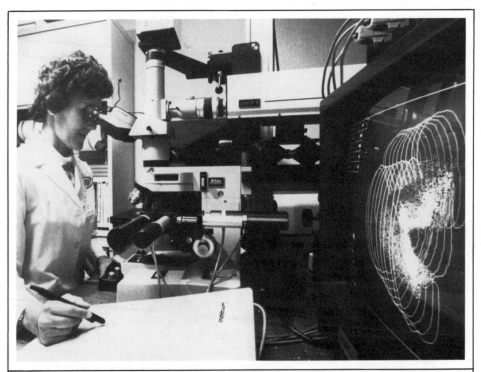

This computer produces a three-dimensional image of brain tissue, enabling researchers to track cellular pathways in the brain.

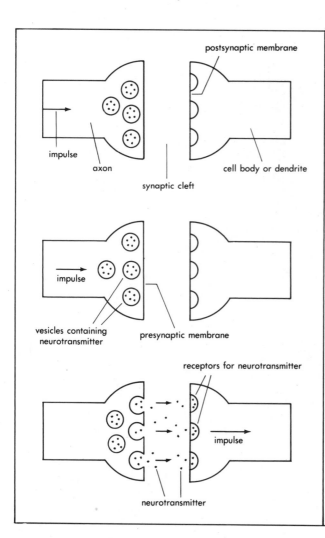

postsynaptic membrane

impulse

axon

synaptic cleft

cell body or dendrite

impulse

vesicles containing
neurotransmitter

presynaptic membrane

receptors for neurotransmitter

impulse

neurotransmitter

Neurotransmitters convey information from cell to cell by crossing the synapses (gaps) between neurons. Drugs can stimulate or inhibit the function of neurotransmitters, causing radical alterations in the mind and body.

But how exactly do neurotransmitters act? Only since the 1950s have scientists understood that the molecules of neurotransmitters fit geometrically into special areas of nerve cells called *receptors*. These receptors accept the molecule that matches their own shape most closely, just as one jigsaw puzzle piece fits together with another that has a particular shape.

Between the ending of one nerve cell, with its storage granules, and the beginning of another nerve cell, with its receptor sites, is a microscopic space called the *synaptic cleft*. To send a chemical message, the storage granules of the first nerve release a neurotransmitter. The neurotrans-

A snake ready to strike is but one of many menaces that prompt the brain to release norepinephrine, a stimulant neurotransmitter that triggers the "fight or flight" response to danger.

mitter molecules move across the synaptic cleft until they reach the receptor sites on the adjoining nerve cell. When the neurotransmitter "plugs" into its specialized receptors into that cell, the signal continues along to the ending of that second cell, where transmission occurs again, to a third cell, and so forth. Ultimately, this produces a biological/chemical pathway made up of nerve cells transmitting and receiving a particular kind of neurotransmitter.

The nature of the neurotransmitter determines how the body will respond to the chemical messages that are being carried. A stimulant neurotransmitter will produce stimulant effects. For example, environmental stress or danger prompts the nerve cells in the brain to release norepinephrine, a stimulant neurotransmitter. Norepinephrine is the body's way of shouting "danger!" The body responds by becoming alert: among other things, the heartbeat rate and blood pressure increase. This response is widely known as the "fight or flight" response. Each neurotransmitter produces a unique response.

At about the same time that scientists located receptor sites on nerve endings in the brain, they found that nerve endings in certain parts of the brain had receptor sites that matched heroin, morphine, or opium molecules. These powerful exogenous drugs fit into these natural, internal receptor sites like a key fits into a lock.

The existence of specific *opiate receptors* raised a perplexing question: Why had the brain developed receptors for opiate drugs?

Various research groups speculated that if the body already contained opiate receptors, it must make its own opiate-like drugs to match these receptors, just as dopamine or serotonin matched other receptors.

In 1975, such a group of body-made opiates was discovered. These biochemicals were named *endorphins*. Endorphins are similar in chemical composition to drugs made from opium; they can even be addictive, as opiates can be.

Dr. Karl Verebey, director of Clinical Pharmacology at the New York State Division of Substance Abuse, describes endorphins as "the brain's shock absorbers." They help cush-

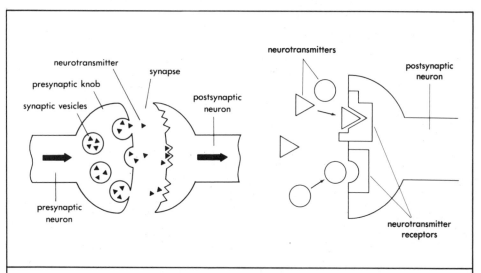

The drawing on the left shows how one neuron signals another across the synapse between them by emitting neurotransmitters. The illustration on the right shows how each kind of neurotransmitter fits into only one kind of receptor on the target neuron.

A victim of catatonic schizophrenia, one of the most debilitating of all mental illnesses. Psychiatric drugs can sometimes control the symptoms of this disease, but they cannot cure the disease itself.

ion and maintain the body's emotional balance, or *homeostasis*, by producing feelings of calm and tranquility. Especially after reactions to stress, they absorb some of the powerful signals sent by the body.

Because endorphins moderate other powerful signals as well, Dr. Verebey describes them as "neuromodulators." Without endorphins, we might swing wildly from one emotional extreme to the other, at the mercy of the neurotransmitters in our brains.

Treating Mental Illness

Many of the psychoactive drugs developed by pharmaceutical corporations since the 1950s imitate or block the body's own neurotransmitters, or interact with the neurotransmitter system to alter brain activity. A group of drugs known as the *antipsychotics*, for example, blocks dopamine receptor sites.

By acting in this way, they stop some of the effects dopamine would have in the brain if it were released normally (agitation, hyperstimulation).

Other drugs cause neurotransmitters to leak out of the nerve cell endings where they are stored, and still other drugs may block enzymes from chemically breaking down a neurotransmitter after it has been used, thereby prolonging its action in the brain or nervous system. (A group of antidepressant drugs called *monoamine oxidase inhibitors* works in this way.)

The discoveries made about brain function in the past 60 years have not only revolutionized our view of the body, they have also revolutionized our power to develop drugs with very sophisticated modes of action to treat humans. The actions and side effects of these drugs, in turn, have clarified scientific knowledge.

Viewed against this background, it is easier to see why "designer drugs" began to appear on the street during the 1980s. Given our advanced knowledge of neurochemistry and neurobiology, designer drugs are a negative, but sophisticated, manifestation of scientific progress.

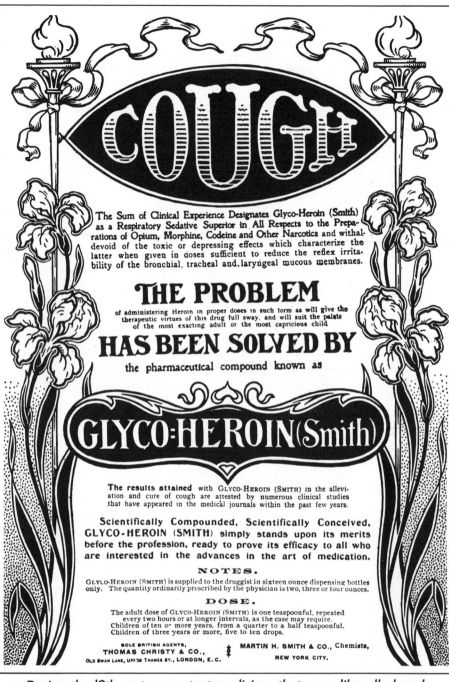

During the 19th century, patent medicines that were liberally laced with heroin and other addictive drugs were sold over the counter. Manufacturers were not required to list their ingredients.

CHAPTER 3

THREE MAJOR
DESIGNER DRUG
GROUPS

The idea of making substitute versions of controlled drugs is not new. In the late 1960s, after the FDA put LSD-25 onto its Schedule I of forbidden drugs, other mind-altering substitutes flooded the underground market. Unfortunately, outlawing a drug does not reduce its supply on the black market as much as it reduces the availability of pure and carefully prepared versions of the drug. This leaves the field open to clumsy, impure, new, and untested drug preparations.

The 1980s saw several new developments in the manufacture of illicit drugs. First was the preparation of illicit synthetic opiates. (The 1960s and 1970s tended to focus on hallucinogens and "basement amphetamines.") Second, computers became much more widely used to store chemical formulas and to search for new psychoactive chemicals; both legitimate and underground chemists had access to this knowledge. Third, more knowledge had been amassed about the brain and the effects drugs have on it. Fourth, there was a growing tendency among drug users to seek out more potent drugs and more synthetic — as opposed to naturally occuring organic—substances.

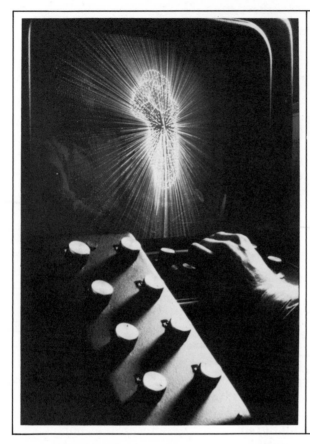

A three-dimensional computer image reveals the molecular structure of a component of DNA. Sophisticated technology allows pharmaceutical companies to refine their products, maximizing desired drug effects and minimizing negative ones.

Designer Opiates

Opium is a botanical drug that occurs naturally in the seeds of some poppies. Thousands of years ago, the ancient Sumerians gathered crude "opium juice" from these seeds to use as medicine. The ancient Greeks dissolved opium in wine as a drug.

In 1805, a German pharmacist isolated the active ingredient in opium and named it *morphine*, after Morpheus, the Greek god of sleep. The name reflects our knowledge that morphine and its compounds cause drowsiness and relaxation along with pain relief.

Diacetylmorphine, a semisynthetic analog of morphine better known as *heroin*, was first synthesized in 1874. This substance did not become known to physicians or the general public in the United States until almost 25 years later. In 1898, chemists at the Bayer Company also synthesized di-acetylmorphine. Heroin was two and a half times more potent than morphine. Ironically, it was originally expected to be a nonaddictive substitute for morphine. During the late 19th century, various potions laced with heroin were widely available in the United States. Not until 1914, when the government passed the Harrison Narcotics Act, was the use of heroin brought under strict regulation.

The most important medical use of morphine and its compounds has always been to treat pain, and they remain the most valuable drugs modern medicine has at its disposal for this purpose. But, although we now know that morphine and its relatives "plug into" opiate receptors in parts of the brain that are heavily involved in carrying "pain transmission"

A medieval depiction of Morpheus, the Greek god of sleep, for whom morphine is named. An analgesic that is derived from opium, morphine is both an effective pain reliever and a highly addictive drug.

signals, we still do not understand why this should reduce pain itself. (After all, these drugs do not block the pain signals running through nerves in the rest of the body, before they reach the brain.) Instead, opiates seem to reduce the emotional elements of pain (fear, anxiety) in an area of the brain called the *thalamus*, and in other parts of the brain as well. In a sense, opiates make the mind indifferent to physical pain. The trouble is that along with their superb analgesic qualities, all drugs derived from opiates can cause physical addiction.

During the 20th century, pharmaceutical corporations have tried to create synthetic drugs that relieve pain as well as the opiates do, but without causing addiction. But no such drug has yet been found. The power of painkilling drugs seems to relate closely to their addictive power.

Why should this be so? Why does narcotic pain relief "fit" together with narcotic addiction? Part of the reason seems to be that opiates fill the same receptors that the body's endorphins do. One explanation for addiction is that prolonged opiate use causes the body to stop producing its own opiates. If this were so, the body's own endorphin supply would be depleted by the time an externally supplied opiate were withdrawn, creating a craving for more of the synthetic substitute that set the depletion process into action in the first place.

Another current theory for addiction is that people who become addicted lack a healthy supply of endorphins from birth. The synthetic narcotic then fills the biological need for homeostasis. (This biological theory of addiction contradicts judgmental theories of addiction, which write off the victims of addiction as being "weak" or "degenerate.") If heroin addiction could in fact be traced to abnormalities in brain chemistry, this would bolster the case for supplying opiates to certain addicts, under medical supervision, just as we now supply insulin to diabetics whose bodies cannot make their own supply of this vital sugar-controlling hormone.

Fentanyl is an example of a synthetic *opioid* drug. Although it is about 200 times as potent as morphine, and has a different chemical structure, it duplicates many of morphine's actions. Fentanyl also stimulates the same opiate receptors in the brain as heroin and morphine, which means that theoretically, an opiate addict could use any of these drugs interchangeably in order to avoid painful withdrawal symptoms.

Furthermore, if an addict develops *tolerance* — the physiological need to take increasingly higher doses of an opiate such as fentanyl to achieve the original effect of the drug — he or she also becomes tolerant to all other drugs in the same class.

Because the effect of fentanyl lasts only about half an hour, many researchers originally assumed that its abuse potential would be lower than that of morphine, on the assumption that addicts would prefer a longer-lasting opiate. However, manufacturers of designer versions of fentanyl shrewdly took its short action into account, and built a longer duration of action into the analogs, with the goal of making their product more appealing to heroin addicts.

The first fentanyl analog to hit the street was alpha-methyl-fentanyl, with a slightly longer-lasting effect and greater potency than its parent drug. This variation, sold as a snowy-white powder, soon became known as "China White." Para-fleuro-fentanyl, alpha-acetyl-fentanyl, and finally 3-methyl-fentanyl (about 100 times as potent as heroin, and with effects lasting nearly as long) all followed. Each of these drugs appeared after the FDA and state legislatures had outlawed the previous one.

Meperidine (sold legally under the trade name Demerol) is, like fentanyl, also a synthetic opioid, in use since 1939. Its medical effects resemble those of morphine, including pain reduction, drowsiness, relaxation, and occasionally constipation. (Interestingly, meperidine dilates the pupils of the eyes, whereas most narcotics contract the pupils to "pinpoints.") It is also addictive, and like fentanyl, produces some cross-tolerance with morphine and heroin. Currently, meperidine is the opiate doctors prescribe most frequently for pain relief for hospitalized patients.

Designer Hallucinogens

MDMA, or Ecstasy, was originally developed before World War I. In the late 1930s, Smith, Kline, and French, an American pharmaceutical company, rejected this drug as a possible commercial appetite suppressant because it caused nausea as a side effect.

methamphetamine

3, 4-methylenedioxyamphetamine
(MDA)

3, 4-methylenedioxymethamphetamine
(MDMA, "Ecstasy")

3, 4-methylenedioxyethamphetamine
(MDEA, "Eve")

Molecular drawings of the designer hallucinogens MDA, MDMA, and MDEA show their structural similarities to methamphetamine, a form of speed. They also resemble mescaline, a natural hallucinogen.

One of the parent drugs of Ecstasy is MDA, a compound belonging to a group of *psychedelic* (mind-altering) substances chemically related to spices such as nutmeg and mace. MDA surfaced in the underground drug market in the mid-1960s as an alternative to LSD, and was known as the "love drug." The FDA put MDA onto its forbidden Schedule I in 1970, at which point manufacturers and users of the drug searched for a legal analog with effects similar to those produced by MDA. The resulting analog was MDMA, which remained legal until 1985.

MDMA is a product of the chemical combination of MDA and methamphetamine. However, MDMA produces less stimulation than cocaine or amphetamines, and it is taken for its hallucinogenic rather than stimulant properties. Users claim it deepens their empathy for others, fosters significant verbal communication, heightens sensory perceptions, and enhances self-awareness.

MDMA is not quite a "classic" hallucinogen, though. The extreme, sometimes frightening, perceptual changes associated with LSD, for example, tend not to occur with MDMA. Furthermore, it has been designed to produce a shorter "trip" than either MDA or LSD. Finally, users of MDMA can, if necessary, function rationally while using it. Perhaps one way to describe this drug is to call it a "domesticated" version of some of the stronger psychedelic agents.

One such stronger psychedelic agent is the drug phencyclidine, better known as PCP. Dr. Charles Schuster, director of the National Institute on Drug Abuse, reporting on designer drugs to the U.S. House of Representatives in May, 1986, said that PCP was "perhaps a prototype for the designer drug problem we now face." His words refer partly to the fact that PCP was originally intended as a pharmaceutical drug for use in a medical setting. It was invented and tested by Parke-Davis, an American pharmaceutical corporation, in the late 1950s, for use as an anesthetic, with the goal of avoiding some of the side effects of other anesthetics — specifically a slowed rate of breathing and *bradycardia* (an abnormally slow heart beat) — and in fact it is effective in maintaining the breathing and heart rates.

Some patients, however, reported that PCP caused frightening dreams or hallucinations during or after surgery. As Ronald Linder and coauthors point out in their book *PCP: The Devil's Dust*, male patients recovering from phencyclidine anesthesia behaved aggressively or violently, and needed several hours of post-surgical supervision. Women were more likely to appear giggly or intoxicated.

Parke-Davis withdrew the drug from the pharmaceutical market because of these odd side effects, but reintroduced it two years later as a veterinary anesthetic. At about the same time, it appeared on San Francisco streets under the abbreviation "PCP" (for Peace Pill), where it quickly developed a reputation as a bizarre, unpredictable drug.

After PCP developed its bad reputation, unscrupulous dealers throughout the United States began to misrepresent PCP as being any of several other drugs. Because some users feared PCP, dealers lied and sold it as LSD, mescaline, or THC (a derivative of marijuana), or sprinkled it on low-grade marijuana to "strengthen" the latter drug. Since pure LSD, mescaline, and THC were rare and expensive in the early 1970s, it is likely that a whole generation of users blamed the grotesque effects of PCP on these far more predictable hallucinogenic drugs. Since one of the greatest risks of PCP comes from using it accidentally or unintentionally, misrepresenting PCP as other drugs was extremely dangerous.

Ultimately, however, some users grew to enjoy the bizarre effects of PCP, and in the late 1970s the drug resurfaced under its real name. At about the same time, analogs of PCP (TCP, PHP, and PCC) were found in several states. These analogs were originally legal, although more potent than and as unpredictable as PCP.

Although scientists do not yet understand how PCP or its analogs affect neurotransmission in the brain, they do know that the effects are dose-dependent. Low doses produce mild stimulant effects, moderate doses distort reality and pain and touch perception, and high doses cause coma and possible psychosis. Because PCP builds up in the brain's fatty tissue and is released slowly, its chronic use may cause effects related to its accumulation in the brain.

Designer Stimulants

Amphetamines are a chemical series of synthetic drugs developed in the 1920s and 1930s. *Cocaine*, on the other hand, is a natural product derived from the leaves of the South American coca plant. South American Indians in the Andes Mountains have chewed coca leaves for thousands of years to combat fatigue and hunger, but the powdered and crystalline forms of this botanical drug produce much stronger effects, making the cocaine sold today in the United States a radically different substance from coca itself.

Although the chemical formulas of cocaine and the amphetamines differ, they affect the brain and body in similar ways. They are both potent *psychomotor stimulants*, meaning that they stimulate mental processes and physical activity. (Cocaine is supposed to be the most potent antifatigue agent known to man.) Socially, their similarity has led to alternating "waves" of amphetamine and cocaine use in the United States since the 1940s, the relative popularity of each depending upon which drug is more readily available at a given time.

A Bolivian woman harvests coca leaves, which have mild psychoactive properties. Cocaine is derived from coca, and its effects are far stronger than those of the botanical drug itself.

The discovery and use of amphetamines as stimulants was quite accidental. In the early 1920s, a Chinese scientist working at the University of California at Los Angeles (UCLA) returned to China to investigate traditional herbal medicines. Intrigued by references to a desert plant, *mahuang*, he tracked the plant down and discovered that scientists had already isolated its active ingredient, *ephedrine*, which is still used today to relieve asthma.

A team of researchers at UCLA, looking for a synthetic substitute for ephedrine, then began to synthesize a chemical series of analogs of it. The "best" analog in their first series was *amphetamine*. Subsequent analogs included *dextroamphetamine* and *methamphetamine*.

Although they were originally designed as synthetic anti-asthma agents, the amphetamines showed other fascinating effects. They increased alertness, seemed to improve mental and physical performance, and reduced fatigue and appetite. In the coming years, amphetamines were to be used medically as antidepressants, weight-reducing agents, and to treat hyperactive children, with varying results.

Today, the only noncontroversial medical use of amphetamines is in treating the rare disease called *narcolepsy*. People suffering from this condition unexpectedly fall asleep, leaving them vulnerable to potentially dangerous consequences.

Initially, the more scientists learned about amphetamines, the more the drug's effects seemed to parallel those of cocaine. Amphetamines seemed to have two advantages, however. Unlike cocaine, they could be taken by mouth and be effectively absorbed by the body, and their effects lasted longer, by about seven hours, than those of cocaine. It is for these reasons, perhaps, that amphetamine use was popular with soldiers of all armies during World War II.

But like most other drugs, amphetamines do have side effects that can range from mildly unpleasant to extremely dangerous.

Cocaine and amphetamines achieve their effects by triggering the release of dopamine and norepinephrine from nerve endings, and preventing the nerve storage sites for these neurotransmitters from reabsorbing them, so that they linger in the synaptic clefts between nerve cells. The net effect is to stimulate all of the dopamine and norepinephrine pathways in the brain. Since these pathways make their way through the parts of the brain that control the highest functions of the mind, mood, feeling, and thought are all affected by the amphetamines. Outside the central nervous system, in the *peripheral nervous system*, which transmits signals from the brain to all other parts of the body, stimulant activity also increases. The lungs expand, the heart speeds up, and blood pressure rises.

Like amphetamines, cocaine also blocks nerve endings that would normally reabsorb dopamine and norepinephrine. At the same time that it is effectively increasing the neurotransmitter action of dopamine by doing this, cocaine inter-

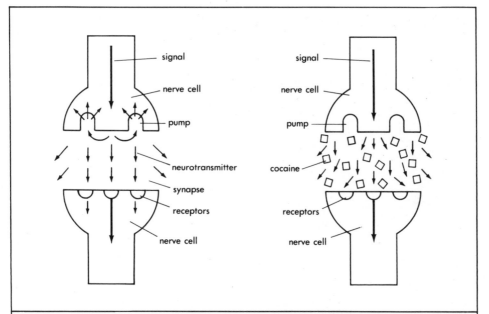

Cocaine works by blocking the return of norepinephrine and dopamine to their cells of origin. This produces a range of feelings from euphoria to anger and depression.

cepts important feedback signals that would normally tell the brain to stop making and releasing dopamine. It also lowers the concentration of serotonin, which would normally cushion the raw effects of dopamine, and it prolongs the time that dopamine spends in the synaptic clefts between nerves. All of these extreme changes in the brain's normal chemical balance cause *hyperstimulation* (overstimulation).

This excess of stimulation has more than one effect. First, it causes *euphoria*, an exaggerated feeling of well-being. However, prolonged use of cocaine and amphetamines also depletes the body of its neurotransmitter "reserves," which can cause extreme depression — the very opposite of these stimulants' pleasurable effects.

When cocaine is smoked, the intensity and speed of its effects on the brain rival those of an intravenous injection: they are about ten times stronger than those of cocaine that is "snorted" through the nose. Cocaine that can be smoked is known on the street as "crack." Crack is not a synthetic

CRACK

SHATTERS LIVES

A poster highlights the dangers of crack. This drug is especially pernicious because it is cheap and relatively easy to use, and therefore appealing to young people.

analog of cocaine. It is a "redesigned" form of cocaine. In this strict sense, crack is not a designer drug.

However, we include crack as a designer drug because the way in which dealers prepare it for smoking substantially changes its effects. Crack has a more intense effect, is more addictive in a shorter period of time, and has more dangerous side effects than does snorted cocaine.

Dealers sell crack in little, ready-to-smoke "rocks." These rocks can approach purity levels of 60 to 80 percent, much higher than the usual purity of snorted or injected cocaine. The purity, as well as the smoking of crack, increases its potency.

Crack appeals to users who are afraid of needles and who do not like the idea of snorting cocaine. This group includes a high percentage of young or relatively innocent users.

This new way of preparing cocaine is a bonanza for dealers. It has vastly expanded the new-user market; moreover, the rapid, high addiction rate of crack (occurring in less than six weeks of beginning regular use) guarantees dealers steady, return customers.

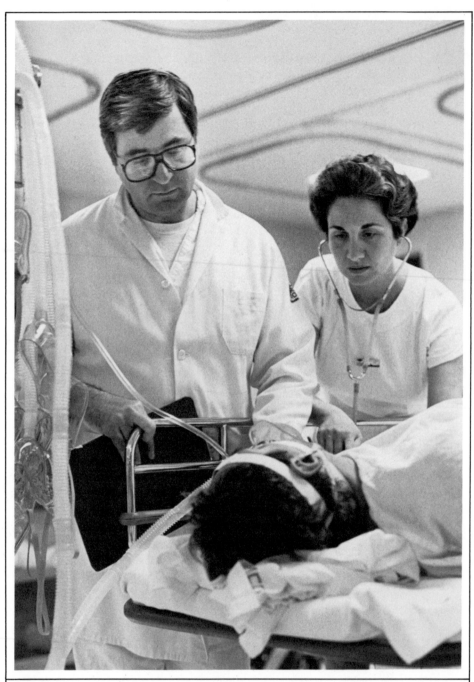

A medical team monitors a patient recovering from surgery. Fentanyl, an anesthetic used in surgery, is one of the most powerful of all drugs, and is safe only in the hands of highly trained professionals.

CHAPTER 4

SIDE EFFECTS OF DESIGNER DRUGS

All drugs have side effects. Usually, drug reactions are described in terms of both the desired *main effect* and these unwanted side effects. But from the user's point of view, one person's side effect can be another person's main effect. If a physician gives a narcotic to reduce pain, for example, he may consider drowsiness a side effect. To the patient receiving the drug, drowsiness may become the desired effect.

When phencyclidine (PCP) was developed as an anesthetic, side effects such as a distorted body image and dreamlike experiences caused the manufacturer to withdraw it from the pharmaceutical market. Recreational users of PCP later sought out the drug for precisely these side effects.

In this chapter, however, the side effects we discuss are any effects of designer drugs that are physically or mentally frightening, damaging, or potentially deadly.

In the 16th century, the European physician Paracelsus (1493–1541) wrote: "All drugs are poisons. What distinguishes a poison from a remedy is the right dose." This statement still holds true. The right dose must take into account a person's sex, height, weight, general physical condition, and age. Elderly people, for example, are more sensitive to most drugs than young people. The right dose of an antihyperten-

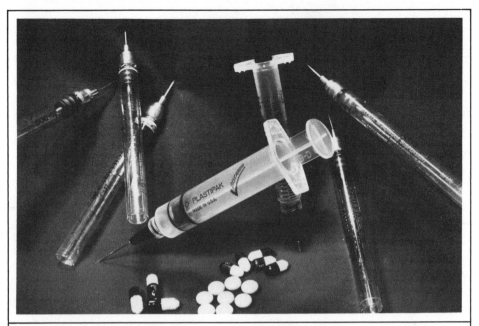

Drugs and assorted drug paraphernalia. The effects of all drugs are closely related to the amount taken and the method of ingestion.

sive (drug that lowers blood pressure) for a patient in his thirties may be too high for an elderly patient. Women, as a rule, are smaller and lighter than men, and may need smaller doses of a given drug.

Many side effects are dose-related. Drugs behave differently according to how large an amount is taken. With most drugs, the likelihood of adverse side effects increases as the dose increases. The point at which the side effects take over from main effects usually happens once a particular dose is reached.

These effects can be physical or mental, major or minor. They may be short, lasting only as long as the drug is in the body, or long, lasting up to a lifetime. They may be reversible or irreversible.

Drugs can be swallowed, inhaled, or injected. They can be rubbed on the skin or inserted into the rectum or vagina as suppositories. These "modes of administration" produce differing results. Some ways of taking a drug can have their own side effects — different and more dangerous than those of the drug itself.

Shared needles or syringes, for example, can transmit hepatitis, other blood infections, and AIDS (acquired immune deficiency syndrome). The bacteria or viruses causing these infections remain on the tips of needles or in the syringes discarded by an infected user, so that the next user injects these microorganisms into his or her bloodstream.

"Set" and "setting" also influence side effects. "Set" refers to the positive or negative mental expectations with which a person approaches a drug. Guilt or fear about using an illicit drug can make the experience disturbing. Similarly, the belief that a drug will "help" a patient can produce beneficial effects. "Setting" includes the people and environment surrounding the person taking a drug.

Still other side effects are caused by interactions between drugs and other substances. Before prescribing a drug, a physician should ask if a patient is taking any other drugs. He or she should also inquire about the patient's diet, since some drugs interact chemically with certain foods.

One example of drug–food interaction involves a group of *antidepressant* drugs called MAO inhibitors that inhibit production of the enzyme monoamine oxidase, or MAO. Patients taking these drugs must avoid avocados, Chianti wine, chocolate, pickled herring, chicken livers, tenderized meats, most cheeses (especially blue cheese, Brie, or Camembert), caviar, and sausages. All of these foods contain a substance called *tyramine*. Normally, MAO metabolizes tyramine, but if the enzyme is inhibited by an MAO-inhibitor-type antidepressant drug, the tyramine from these foods remains active in the body, where it may cause headache, rapid heartbeat, and an increase in blood pressure that can rupture blood vessels and cause bleeding inside the skull. In extreme cases, the interaction between MAO inhibitors and tyramine in restricted foods can result in a stroke or even death.

Fentanyl Analogs

Fentanyl and its analogs are 40 to several thousand times more *active* (potent) than morphine. This degree of activity increases the danger of overdose with fentanyl. Under the best of conditions (in surgery, for example), fentanyl occasionally causes a *spasm*, or muscular contraction, of the chest muscles, along with very slow breathing. Together, these side effects can stop breathing.

In a hospital setting, anesthetists can quickly administer artificial ventilation and drugs to relax the chest muscles in such an emergency. On the street, however, or at home, where such options are unavailable, overdose with fentanyl becomes an obvious danger.

In terms of physical side effects, fentanyl addiction is dangerous because it causes *tolerance*. Tolerance refers to the way the body first gets used to, and then needs, a particular drug. As addiction to opiates develops, the nerve endings "welcome" drugs that fit its opiate receptors. Eventually, larger and more frequent doses of the drug are needed to produce the effects of the original, smaller doses. As the dose needed increases as a result of tolerance, the danger of overdose also increases. In addition, with higher doses, all the opioid side effects become more pronounced. These include

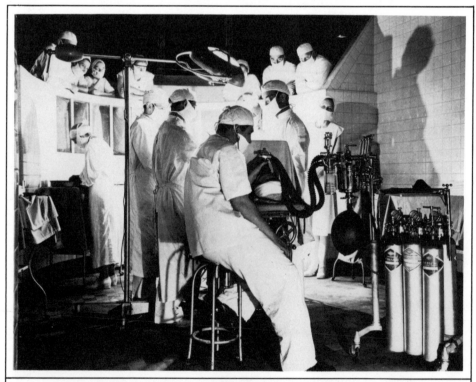

An anesthesiologist monitors his patient during surgery. If a drug-induced emergency occurs, his intervention could be life-saving.

An addict suffers the agonies of withdrawal syndrome. Withdrawal from fentanyl produces symptoms similar to those of withdrawal from heroin, including chills, sweating, cramps, nausea, and panic.

slurred speech, slowed thinking, slowed reflexes, and withdrawal of interest in the outside world.

Taking an opioid drug away from an addict, on the other hand, precipitates a group of side effects called the *withdrawal syndrome*. These effects occur, for example, if an addict cannot obtain drugs. Withdrawal from fentanyl analogs causes symptoms like those of withdrawal from heroin, including chills and sweating, cramps, nausea, irritability, panic, insomnia, and anorexia. These side effects are usually not life-threatening, but they are extremely uncomfortable.

MDMA

Because MDMA (Ecstasy) resembles both of its "parent" compounds — methamphetamine and MDA — it produces similar side effects. These effects include loss of appetite, nausea, insomnia after the drug effect has worn off, jaw-clenching, and general restlessness, all of which are also common side effects of amphetamine use. Journalist P. J. O'Rourke described his reaction to MDMA in a 1985 article for *Rolling Stone* magazine: "To me, it felt like a very sophisticated, extremely well-buffered speed." Anyone with high blood pressure or a heart condition should be especially careful to avoid a drug with stimulant side effects.

Long before the FDA put MDMA on its Schedule I, a team of scientists at the University of Chicago studied its effects on rats. They found that animals fed MDA at different doses all showed low levels of the neurotransmitter serotonin in their brains, which in the case of this drug was caused by an actual degeneration of the nerves that contain serotonin. Subsequent studies by other researchers have shown that MDMA produces the same effect as MDA.

Such results point to physical brain damage as a possible irreversible side effect of MDMA use. Partly as a result of these studies, the FDA put MDMA on Schedule I in late 1985.

PCP and Its Analogs

PCP's effects vary enormously with the dose, set, setting, and personality of the user. Keeping in mind that phencyclidine was meant to be used as an anesthetic drug, the reasons for

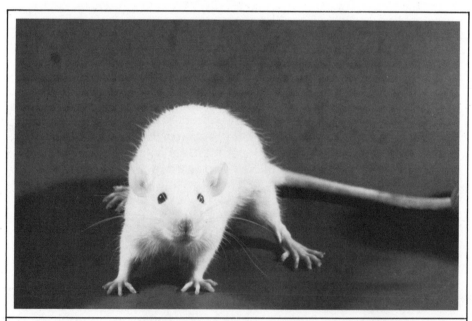

Research on laboratory rats revealed that MDA lowers the level of serotonin in the brain by destroying the nerve cells that produce this neurotransmitter. MDMA has proved to have the same effect.

some of the bizarre side effects that occur when it is used as a mind-altering drug become clear. What was meant to be an anesthetic with mind-altering side effects becomes a mind-altering drug with anesthetic side effects.

At low doses (1 to 5 milligrams) of PCP most users claim that they feel less inhibited, and that their conversation has greater significance. Their sense of the passage of time slows down, and *synesthesia* — or translation of one sense into another, as when people "hear" colors or "see" music — may occur.

More serious side effects begin to occur at higher doses (5 to 10 milligrams and up), nearer the doses given for anesthetic purposes. These side effects include

•Loss of behavior control. PCP reduces inhibitions in much the same way that the *sedative-hypnotics* (drugs that induce relaxation and sleep) do. However, it also stimulates aggressive drives, just as cocaine and amphetamines do. Simultaneously, PCP begins to distort reality in a unique way. Pain and touch perception decrease, signaling the onset of anesthesia. The body image changes so that the user may feel enormous, or as if he is "swimming through glue," or as if his body is unrelated to his mind. The brain no longer organizes information about the outside world efficiently. Judgment, self-observation, even the sense of self can disappear at high doses.

•The "eyes open coma." At high doses, PCP induces unconsciousness, even though the victim's eyes may still be open. Blood pressure, heart rate, and the rate of breathing are all up — an advantage for a drug used as an anesthetic agent, but also dangerous to the body. The coma can alternate with bursts of extremely destructive activity.

•Aggression and violence. One reason such destructive behavior can occur at high doses is that the brain can no longer understand the environment. A noisy environment, filled with stimuli or movement, may be so confusing to a PCP user that he or she may lash out randomly. Furthermore, since the user has little touch or pain perception left, violence that might exhaust or hurt a drug-free individual has little effect on a PCP user.

•Post-PCP amnesia and depression. Someone who has received high doses of PCP may not remember the experience, because from a medical point of view, he or she was unconscious while it lasted. This may explain why some people continue to use this drug after an adverse reaction. With chronic PCP use, long-term depression can occur.

Cocaine and Crack

The side effects of smoked cocaine, or crack, resemble those of injected cocaine or amphetamines taken in high doses.

Crack is a powerful *vasoconstrictor*, a substance that narrows the blood vessels. It drives up the pressure needed to push blood through the body. If the blood pressure rises enough, it can burst a blood vessel in the brain, causing a *stroke*. Crack also makes the heart beat faster, which in some cases causes a heart attack.

Chronic use of crack can also result in *cocaine psychosis*. Victims of cocaine psychosis are agitated and suspicious of their environment and the people around them. Sometimes they feel that bugs are crawling under their skin. They may also experience *tactile hallucinations*, or feeling things that are not there.

Cocaine psychosis takes months or years to develop in someone who snorts cocaine, but in compulsive crack users, it can develop in a few weeks.

In the early 1980s, many responsible researchers claimed that cocaine was not physically addictive. There are several reasons why they may have underestimated its addictive potential. First, cocaine addiction does not resemble addiction to opiates. As far as we know, there is no "lock-and-key" fit between a cocaine molecule and a nerve receptor, as there is between an opiate molecule and an opiate receptor. Instead, cocaine stimulates the "reward centers" of the brain. The addiction takes the form of a compulsion to keep taking cocaine in order to keep stimulating these parts of the brain.

Second, the withdrawal syndrome also appears to be different. Withdrawal from opiates leaves the addict raw and irritable. Withdrawal from crack leaves the addict depressed, exhausted, and *anhedonic*, or unable to take the slightest pleasure from anything.

Third, an opiate addict with steady access to his or her drug is actually "reasonably" functional, may hold a job, and can maintain physical stability. In other words, the most noticeable side effects develop with loss of the drug. For a cocaine addict, the reverse is true. Cocaine psychosis develops because a user has steady access to cocaine.

There are, however, similarities in tolerance — one of the hallmarks of physical addiction — between cocaine and narcotics addiction. Crack addicts need more and more cocaine to reproduce the same degree of high, just as opiate addicts need more and more opiate over time to reproduce their high. Needless to say, the more cocaine an addict takes, the greater the risk of increasingly severe side effects.

Although these side effects can be uncomfortable and in some cases life-threatening, they are in many ways "predictable." Some designer drugs, if synthesized or mixed incorrectly, can have far more unpredictable effects than cocaine. In these cases, the user pays the price for experimenting with drugs produced with little or no quality control, and the results can be tragic—even fatal.

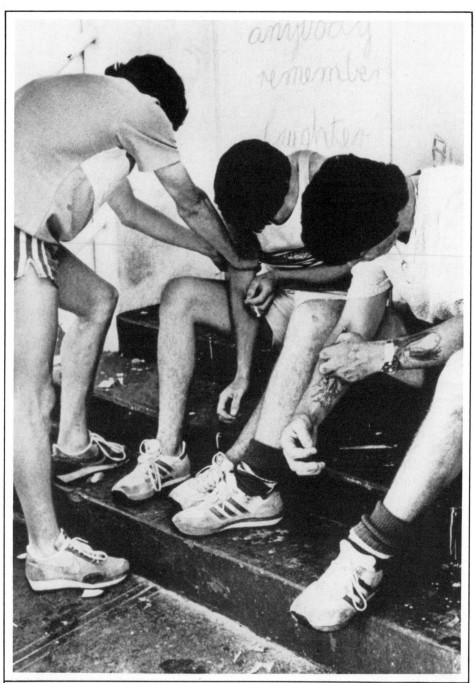

Young addicts mainline heroin in Sydney, Australia. Drug abuse has always carried with it the risks of addiction, disease, and death. Designer drugs increase these risks dramatically.

CHAPTER 5

TWO CAUTIONARY TALES FROM THE STREET

We usually associate young people with the height of physical beauty and grace. But several young people in northern California who used a "synthetic heroin" have no youth left.

Chronologically, they are still young — from age 20 to their early 40s. But they sit hunched over, in some cases literally "frozen stiff." They resemble elderly patients with end-stage Parkinson's disease.

In fact, they do have Parkinson's disease, which is a chronic neurological disorder that usually occurs in the elderly. Its main symptoms are rigidity, tremor, and difficulty in moving. The main abnormality of the brain in this disease is damage to the *substantia nigra*, an area of the brain that helps control voluntary movement. To eat, speak, move, or smile, victims of parkinsonism require powerful medications such as *levadopa* or *carbidopa*. These medications cause ugly and distressing side effects themselves, such as rolling movements of the entire body.

The young patients in California are not biological freaks. They are addicts who injected a designer drug they thought was a "new heroin." It destroyed part of their brains.

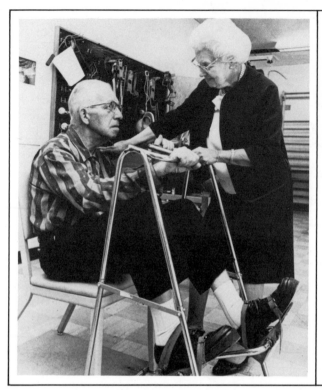

An elderly victim of Parkinson's disease undergoes physical therapy. Young drug abusers in California were stricken with Parkinson-like symptoms when they took a designer drug contaminated by the neurotoxin MPTP.

As many as 400 other addicts who injected this drug have identified themselves. They have milder symptoms or no symptoms at all. But they too may develop Parkinson's disease at a very early age. Here is how it happened.

MPPP (its chemical name is 1-methyl-4-phenyl-4-proprionoxy-piperidine) is a chemical whose structure is closely related to that of the drug Demerol (the brand name for meperidine).

Meperidine is a useful *analgesic* (painkiller) manufactured by the American drug company Winthrop Breon. It is an opiate drug related to other opiates such as morphine and heroin. Like all opiates, Demerol is a potent pain reliever that causes euphoria and is addictive.

The FDA classifies Demerol as a Schedule II drug. This means that Demerol is medically useful, but can cause addiction. Consequently, a prescription for Demerol must be written and signed by a doctor. The prescription can be refilled only with a doctor's written approval, and supplies of the drug are kept under lock and key.

At the time of the California drug disaster cited above, MPPP was *not* controlled in this way. Anyone could legally manufacture, sell, or use it, even though it is closely related to and more powerful than Demerol.

Sometime in 1976 in California, a graduate chemistry student with a history of drug problems (he had become addicted to Demerol after a painful car accident) began to synthesize MPPP in his home lab. He told his mother he was trying to develop a nonaddictive form of Demerol.

At some point in 1977, after having injected MPPP into himself without damage for several months, the student probably tried to simplify the chemical synthesis of the drug. Perhaps he heated the *precursor materials* (chemicals used to make MPPP) at too high a temperature, hoping to speed up the process. In any case, instead of MPPP he produced a toxic chemical—MPTP.

It was a simple mistake, but Nature rarely forgives mistakes. In the brain, MPTP is changed into a deadly *neurotoxin*, or poison that attacks nerve cells. It destroys cells in the substantia nigra.

The student developed symptoms of parkinsonism, very unusual in young people. The following year, after dying from an overdose of an unknown drug, he was autopsied and found to have suffered from parkinsonism. Very few nerve cells remained in the substantia nigra of his brain.

In 1978 his doctor, Glenn Davis, M.D., as a result of research he conducted at the National Institute of Mental Health, published a report on the case, in *Psychiatry Research* magazine. There the story gathered dust until the summer of 1982.

Then in July 1982, a heroin addict entered Santa Clara Valley Medical Center in San Jose, California, hardly able to move or speak. A week later the addict's girlfriend arrived with similar symptoms. Both had tried a "new heroin" a couple of weeks earlier.

Although their "frozen" postures suggested parkinsonism, their physicians, William Langston, M.D., and Phillip Ballard, M.D., did not seriously consider this diagnosis at first. After all, Parkinson's is a "geriatric disease," and these addicts were young. Why would they have a disease of elderly people?

While visiting a friend's house, Dr. Ballard met James Tetrud, M.D., a neurologist from a nearby town. Dr. Tetrud was baffled by two drug users in his care. They, too, had recently shot a "new heroin," and they, too, had become "frozen." The physicians were dealing with similar symptoms. Had the four patients injected the same substance?

Drs. Langston, Ballard, and Tetrud prepared a news release warning of a dangerous new heroin circulating in northern California. At the same time, they sent drug samples supplied by the users to several labs for analysis.

Over the next few days, addicts straggled into the Santa Clara hospital, frightened by the news they had heard.

One *toxicologist* (a chemist who analyzes poisons), a woman named Dr. Halle Weingarten, recalled the article in *Psychiatry Research* describing similar symptoms in a young

William Langston, M.D., was one of the California physicians who unlocked the mysteries of the MPTP catastrophe. Langston also helped broadcast the dangers of this "new heroin" to the public.

A technician examines cultures in a hospital lab. Designer "druggists" lack the expertise of such professionals, and are frequently unaware of the exact composition of their products.

chemistry student synthesizing MPPP. This proved to be the clue to solving the mystery. When the drug samples at the Santa Clara hospital were analyzed as MPTP with traces of MPPP, it seemed clear that the same sloppy lab techniques that had crippled the chemistry student who had made his own MPPP were resulting in increasing supplies of contaminated drugs and a growing number of patients with similar symptoms.

Ironically, three useful developments grew out of this ugly chemical episode. First, in 1985, the FDA moved to reduce private manufacture of MPPP by classifying it as a Schedule I drug. It is now illegal to produce MPPP except for legitimate research purposes.

Second, in late 1986 the U.S. House and Senate passed a bill prohibiting the manufacture of drugs that are structurally similar to Schedule I and Schedule II drugs.

Third, researchers can now produce Parkinson's disease in squirrel monkeys by injecting them with MPTP, which may help them learn how to block the development of parkinsonism in human beings. Because MPTP produces its effects by becoming metabolized or changed chemically in the body into another neurotoxin, scientists hope that by studying this process they can learn how to block the change.

But the crippled addicts are unlikely to benefit any time soon from these experiments. For the moment, their story stops with the symptoms their doctors describe in *Science* magazine:

> Examination of each addict revealed near total immobility, a sharp, generalized increase in muscle rigidity, the inability to speak intelligibly, a fixed stare, facial seborrhea [fatty or oily pimples], constant drooling, and cogwheel rigidity of the arms, [whose movements were jerky, consisting of small jumps like a cogwheel in a bicycle.]

1,000 Times Stronger Than Heroin

Fentanyl, like meperidine, is a useful pharmaceutical developed by a legitimate drug company, Janssen Pharmaceutical. Known by its brand name, Sublimaze, it is a short-acting, potent anesthetic used widely in surgical operations.

Fentanyl's chemical structure is different from that of "natural" opiates like opium, morphine, and heroin, but it has similar opiate actions. Like meperidine, fentanyl is a Schedule II drug, so powerful that even an extra milligram (one-thousandth of a gram) can be fatal.

In the late 1970s, California hospitals began to report cases of addicts who had died of apparent drug overdose. When labs analyzed samples of their blood or tissues, they found no drug. Not until 1981 was the U.S. Drug Enforcement Administration (DEA) laboratory in Washington, D.C., able to identify the killer substance. It was alpha-methyl-fentanyl, an analog of fentanyl. Only two labs in the United States had equipment powerful enough to detect the presence of minute amounts of this derivative of fentanyl in the addicts' blood-streams.

Alpha-methyl-fentanyl was banned in 1981, but before the year had ended, underground chemists had developed a second, still more potent, analog of fentanyl. When this second variation was banned, still newer fentanyl variants surfaced. Because each of these derivatives varied slightly in chemical structure from the preceding drug, each was technically legal until linked to deaths.

Fentanyl analogs are suspected in at least 100 deaths, but the number may be much higher, because the amounts of these drugs are so tiny they are difficult to detect. To prove that someone has used these drugs, tests must be able to

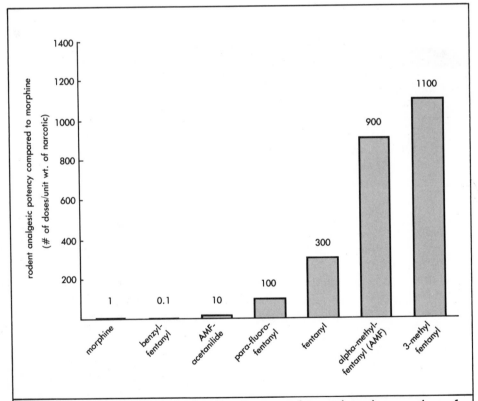

This graph compares the potency of various fentanyl analogs to that of morphine, based on experiments with laboratory rats. Fentanyl is so powerful that even an extra milligram can make a dose fatal.

A block of mannitol, one of the adulterants used to cut fentanyl and its derivatives before they are sold on the streets.

detect about one *nanogram* — one billionth of a gram — in body fluids.

The same quality that makes fentanyl derivatives dangerous — their *potency* — makes these drugs easy to transport and highly profitable. A small amount of pure drug in the lab represents an immense amount of drug on the street — about one million doses per tablespoon — after other substances are added to "cut" the fentanyl derivative.

When something as potent as one of these fentanyl derivatives is cut, large amounts of "cutter" material must be added. The substances used to cut fentanyl analogs include, among others, lactose, mannitol (an infant laxative), or even strychnine, a deadly poison.

Cutting a drug is like sifting together flour and baking powder to make a cake. Most recipes call for a teaspoon or so of baking powder to about two cups of flour. If the baking powder is not thoroughly distributed through the flour, the cake will not rise properly. The result is a flat or unevenly cooked cake.

Similarly, fentanyl derivatives and the substances used to cut them must be thoroughly mixed in order to produce "safe" amounts of the drug per dose. But the amount of cutter needed is vastly greater — hundreds of pounds per *tablespoon* of drug — than the amount of flour that would have to be added to baking powder to make a cake.

If the proportions are wrong, or the substances carelessly mixed, the end result can be death. And as we have seen, the victims, more often than not, are young people out for a good time who wind up paying for it with their health, or even their lives.

A young ballerina with her teacher. The brain and nervous system, so essential to muscular control, are still developing during the teenage years; certain drugs may interfere with that development.

CHAPTER 6

THE SPECIAL STATUS OF ADOLESCENTS

As a group, adolescents are more vulnerable to drug use than adults because they are still growing and changing on their way to maturity. The physical, sexual, emotional and intellectual transformations humans undergo as they mature are called *developmental changes*. Not much hard evidence supports the idea that drug use causes any greater physical damage to adolescents than to adults. But health professionals strongly believe that drugs can delay or distort intellectual or emotional development.

Even after the body reaches its final height, the adolescent brain and nervous system continue to develop. The number of neurons or nerve cells in the central nervous system is complete, but an important process called *myelination* continues. In this process *myelin*, a thin coating of fatty material, grows around the *axon* — the long, thin part of the nerve cell that conducts electrical signals down the nerve cell to the synaptic cleft, where the cell adjoins another nerve cell. Only the nervous systems of higher animals, such as man and the other mammals, have protective myelin coverings around their nerves.

In early childhood, a burst of myelination seems to accompany new learning and coordination skills. Does myelination also accompany new development in adolescence? Does drug use affect myelination? The answers to these questions are still unknown, but there is a real possibility that drug abuse interferes with this crucial process. Moreover, we do know that all of the drugs described in this book affect the nerves and neurotransmitters in the brain and central nervous system. It is therefore reasonable to hypothesize that drugs may have particularly influential effects on the developing nervous system.

Dr. Sidney Cohen suggests (in his book *The Substance Abuse Problems, Volume I*) that the bodies of young people may have more trouble than adults' bodies in breaking down drugs, because some of their enzyme systems (enzymes and proteins that deactivate drugs) may not have matured. But this, too, has yet to be proven.

The Cardiovascular System

The cardiovascular system comprises the heart and blood vessels. Though the brain and central nervous system are still developing during adolescence, the cardiovascular system is usually at its peak in young people. Adolescents have more stamina than adults, and can survive tremendous amounts of physical stress, such as athletic competition. They recover quickly from physical exhaustion.

Crack abuse can destroy this superb efficiency, sometimes permanently. We mentioned in Chapter 4 that stimulants dramatically increase heart rate and blood pressure. Both of these functions usually return to normal when either natural stress or the action of stimulants ends. But in susceptible people (people with a genetic predisposition, heart disease, or stress) — even young people — the blood pressure stays up permanently. Over time, this lasting *hypertension* (high blood pressure) damages the blood vessels and heart, sometimes causing a stroke or heart attack.

Furthermore, babies born to mothers who use crack can have strokes. Some of these infants are hypertensive. Some have had strokes as early as one year of age.

These potential effects of cocaine are considered physical developmental effects, because hypertension, heart dis-

A young runner at the top of her form. Evidence indicates that crack can undermine the normally excellent physical stamina and resiliency of adolescent athletes.

ease, and stroke are not normally associated with youth. They are clear examples of physical damage from drug use that would not have occurred naturally.

Damage to Sexual Function

Most psychoactive drugs have temporary effects on sexuality —either on desire or on orgasm.

Opiates decrease all drives because they depress the functioning of the nervous system. Users typically report a weakened sexual desire and reduced male potency. The potency and desire can return, however, if the user withdraws from these drugs. Women who are addicted to opiates sometimes stop menstruating while addicted, but the normal cycle resumes after drug withdrawal.

Stimulants (including crack) increase drives, including sexuality. The effect ends when the drug action ends. With chronic cocaine use, however, all interests — including sex — tend to become subordinated to the interest in getting and using cocaine.

PCP has a reputation for increasing sexual desire in women, and in some cases delaying male orgasm. However,

PCP can make it more difficult for both men and women to reach orgasm.

MDMA, like other hallucinogens, is reported to be less powerful in increasing the sexual drive than it is sensuous in its effects. An MDMA user, for example, might be less interested in making love to a particular person than in relating emotionally to a tree or appreciating the pattern in a fabric.

All of these effects are reversible, and do not permanently alter sexual function as far as we know. However, for both men and women, sex is not just physical; it is profoundly affected by thought and emotions. We can say that people "bring a lot of luggage to bed" with them. This "luggage" includes nervousness or worry about one's sexual performance, about being loved by one's partner, insecurity about looks, and hopes and expectations about sexual happiness.

If you add to this mix of factors the relative emotional vulnerability of adolescence, and the enormous mood swings that are normal for this period of life, you can see that any drug that affects sexual function makes it harder for the user to know what he or she is really like sexually. And any drug that obscures real desires delays self-discovery.

Adolescence is a time of emotional vulnerability. Drug abuse only adds to the turbulence of these already difficult years.

A poster from the "Just Say No" anti-drug campaign vividly dramatizes the negative impact drugs can have on academic performance.

The Adolescent Mind

During puberty, something very interesting happens to humans. They begin to think more abstractly. Previously incomprehensible intellectual and ethical concepts become clearer. Young people begin to look at the world more critically at this time, and to compare principles with behavior in a logical way.

This is the developmental period when some young people start to show real talent in some given area, be it science, math, art, business, mechanics, or philosophy. Almost everyone, regardless of inherent ability, steps forward in some way during adolescence.

All psychoactive drugs affect thinking, concentration, memory, and perception, sometimes in very subtle ways, and can prevent the appearance and development of these new-found talents.

Amphetamines appeal to some users because they produce feelings of alertness, enhanced mental ability, and greater concentration. They mask the body's fatigue, permitting users to work for extended periods of time. However, they also cause sleeplessness and fatigue the following day. As the effect of an amphetamine wears off, the user's concentration is actually decreased briefly. At a time in life when one's sense of connection to the environment undergoes deep and rapid changes, drugs that undercut one's connection with reality can be especially harmful. An adolescent's sense of identity can be fragile. Mind-altering drugs that can induce confusion, paranoia, and even psychosis have obviously dangerous consequences for a young person's developing sense of him- or herself. With the passage of time, some users of amphetamines and cocaine begin to doubt that they can do good intellectual or creative work without the spur of these stimulants. This is the point at which psychological drug dependence can develop.

Opiates can cause intense drowsiness and "mental clouding," making it impossible to concentrate, register information, or organize thought.

Hallucinogens produce ego and perceptual changes that can range from diverting to fascinating to terrifying. The destructive effects of marijuana on short-term memory have been well documented. Heavy use of marijuana can lead to apathy, confusion, and radical disruption of the learning process. These side effects can deeply disrupt school performance and social development.

Even normal adolescence involves emotional turmoil that would seem abnormal at most other stages of development. Some of the turmoil is expressed in mood swings, abrupt switches of loyalties and opinions, total self-sacrifice, total self-involvement, deceit, extreme honesty, rebellion, submissiveness, brilliance, and stupidity.

These abrupt changes are a form of experimental "play" learning unique to humans, but similar to the useful "play" hunting of lion and tiger cubs. When the dust settles, most people have survived and know more about how to control their emotions, who they are, and how they feel about the opposite sex.

Drug use can definitely complicate this already complicated period of development, or even arrest it completely. In such cases, all of the emotional growth that has been delayed by drug use must be undertaken later — sometimes years later than normal.

Drugs can also intensify mood swings. Of the designer drugs discussed in this book, two — cocaine and PCP — affect mood in particularly destructive ways.

Smokable cocaine (crack) produces rapid alternations between euphoria (the effect of the drug) and depression (the decline of the drug effect). Withdrawal from crack can involve a severe, sometimes lengthy depression. Furthermore, those who take this drug find it very hard to control their emotions. Impulsive and aggressive behavior tends to increase according to how regularly the drug is used. Finally, Dr. Karl Verebey describes cocaine as a "delusionary" drug, meaning that its users often insist they have no problems and that everything is fine, even as their professional and personal worlds crumble around them. The drug deludes them, or allows them to delude themselves, into misreading reality.

The passage from childhood to adulthood involves learning what it means to be a sexual being. Some experts believe that teenage substance abuse delays or halts the development of adult sexuality.

Two preteens share a marijauna cigarette. Children who become chemically dependent are in danger of stunting their emotional and intellectual growth.

We have already mentioned that PCP in high doses tends to precipitate violent or aggressive outbursts. In addition, a study that compared the intellectual skills of PCP users and nonusers suggested that PCP users had the same intellectual abilities as nonusers, but were less able to control their emotions. They reacted to difficult or frustrating questions with emotional outbursts, even though they were not under the influence of the drug at the time. This could mean that PCP has long-term effects on mood, or that people who tend to use PCP are already less able to control their emotions than other people.

Drugs can also lower one's self-esteem. Some quiet, unassuming people turn into "party animals" after drinking a couple of beers. Others display a superb sense of humor under the influence of marijuana. These are "drug-induced" personality changes. The problem with such changes is that they confuse the user and, strangely enough, lower self-esteem rather than raise it. Users may wonder whether their humor or friendliness belong to their own personality or to the drug they are taking. Over time, a user may become convinced that he or she needs the drug to be an impressive personality. This misperception delays self-discovery by causing the user to underestimate his or her own gifts.

Growing Up Is Hard Enough Without Drugs

The "work" of maturing includes sexual, mental, and emotional growth that is much harder to measure than height or weight. Drugs cause their most negative effects in these areas of subtle change, simply because their effects are easier to ignore or belittle than is physical damage to the body.

Drug use can divert attention from the task of growing up. This in itself would not be so terrible if it were possible to take a vacation from reality and make up for lost time later on in life. But the truth is that later, other growth tasks tend to cry out for attention.

In an article published in *Postgraduate Medicine* magazine, Ian MacDonald, M.D., sums up the central problem young drug abusers face: "A child who becomes chemically dependent may never develop adult ethical beliefs. Development of adult sexuality and self identity may be delayed or halted. . . . A [young] patient who has a chronologic age of 18 may have a developmental age of only 13."

Although all drugs can have detrimental effects on adolescents, designer drugs present a particular problem. Because of their unpredictable nature, further complicated by the lack of quality control in their manufacture, designer drugs can, and have, proved tragic to some of their young users.

Unfortunately, designer drugs are available to nearly anyone who wants them. If we cannot stop the demand for these substances, there is little anyone can do to stop their production and sale. Fortunately, the U.S. government has recently taken steps to control and penalize the production and selling of designer drugs, in an effort to fight back against this latest drug problem.

Ronald Reagan hands the pen he used to sign the 1986 Anti-Drug Abuse Act to First Lady Nancy Reagan. Mrs. Reagan's efforts during the 1980s have helped to spur a national campaign against drug abuse.

CHAPTER 7

FIGHTING BACK

During 1985 and 1986, publicity about designer drugs grew. Popular magazines such as *U.S. News & World Report*, *Newsweek*, *Life*, and *Psychology Today* printed articles describing the characteristics and side effects of these drugs. The issue in question at the time was the legality of the drugs produced. Partly because of this publicity, California, the original home of the fentanyl and MPTP disasters, as well as other states, held government hearings on designer drugs.

The hearings, which culminated in reports to Congress, included testimony from the mother of the graduate student who synthesized MPPP.

Ultimately, in late October 1986, the House and Senate passed a bill called the Drug Free America Act of 1986. One section of this bill deals specifically with designer drugs. As of 1987, this is the only federal legislation directed against designer drugs.

The Controlled Substances Analogs Act is part of the larger Drug Free America bill. This act says that a "controlled substance analog" is any substance whose chemical structure is "substantially similar to" the chemical structure of any

Characters from the hit television program "The Cosby Show" urge young people to "help someone to just say no."

substance now included in Schedules I or II. These schedules include drugs such as heroin, mescaline, LSD, THC, marijuana, opium, morphine, cocaine, meperidine, and the amphetamines, as well as MDMA, PCP, and fentanyl.

The act widens the definition of analogs to include substances whose stimulant, hallucinogenic, or depressant effects resemble the effects of substances in Schedules I or II. The hope is that this will discourage underground research on new, chemically different compounds with psychoactive effects.

Furthermore, anyone who manufactures, sells, or uses analogs of controlled drugs now breaks a federal law. The penalties for producing such analogs have also been increased. An individual producing these drugs now faces fines of as much as four million dollars. A drug-ring leader or head manufacturer risks life imprisonment as well. Objections to the Drug Free America bill have already arisen. By giving the

FDA power to outlaw groups of drugs rather than one drug at a time, the bill provides the government with a powerful weapon against underground chemists. But whether it will deter dealers from selling existing drug supplies remains to be seen.

Some psychiatrists and researchers objected when MDMA was included in the Drug Free America bill, because they felt that this drug had therapeutic value and that further research on it should not be curtailed. Putting a drug on the FDA schedules increases the difficulty of conducting research on it, since scientists must then apply to the FDA for permission to make and use the drug.

As Ronald Linder notes in his book *PCP: The Devil's Dust*, legitimate research on the side effects of PCP stopped when it was put on Schedule I, yet the drug continued to be peddled on the street. Thus, by reducing research on PCP, scheduling had the unintended effect of reducing protection of the public against this drug.

Police arrest a man for selling illicit drugs. Before the passage of the Drug Free America Act, which prohibits the manufacture, sale, or use of designer drugs, it was legal to traffic these chemical analogs.

While many people consider this to be a real problem, some pharmacologists respond by pointing out that research grants are not impossible to get, even for research on scheduled drugs, and that the cost for such research is probably counterbalanced by the immediate benefit it brings to the public.

The Drug Free America Act also addresses the special vulnerability of young people to all types of drugs. One section of the act doubles all financial penalties for drug dealers or manufacturers who use children or teenagers as their "runners." (Producers began to use children to "front," or cover for them because it is harder to jail a juvenile than an adult. In addition, an adult exploiting a child in this way avoided risk to himself.)

A second section of the act "requests" that the media and the entertainment industry stop glamorizing drugs, alcohol, and drug-associated criminals, and even start developing materials that discourage drug use.

A third section allocates funds to develop school-based drug education programs. Presumably, this will include courses about drugs for teachers and families as well as for students.

Most of the money allocated by the act, however, goes to support measures meant to reduce drug supplies. The act strongly emphasizes the need to stop drug smuggling into the United States, and calls for increased participation by the U.S. Department of Defense in border patrols and customs checks. In fact, 75 percent of the funds allocated by Congress in this bill will be spent on reducing supplies of drugs, while the remaining 25 percent will go toward reducing the consumer demand for drugs.

One possible weakness of the Drug Free America Act, as of previous U.S. anti-drug legislation, is its tendency to focus on a foreign drug menace, rather than asking Americans to take the responsibility for controlling domestic drug consumption.

Although it is true that foreign drugs smuggled into this country supply a large part of the American drug market, it is equally correct that the incentive to import drugs is supported by American demand for them.

Obviously, if Americans continue to seek drugs to alter, improve, or deny the reality of their lives, someone will surely supply them. Furthermore, if foreign supply is reduced but not domestic demand, the way will be clear for "designer drug" chemists to step in and supply the existing market with synthetic drugs made illegally in America.

In addition, if cheaper, more-easily-come-by substitutes become available in America, demand for foreign drugs will be greatly diminished. There are recent examples in U. S. history to support this theory.

One such recent example was the switch from cocaine to amphetamines during the 1930s. Cocaine use dropped steeply in the 1940s, '50s, and '60s. Edward Brecher, in his book *Licit and Illicit Drugs*, attributes this reduction not to law-enforcement efforts, but to the discovery of amphetamines. After 1932, domestic amphetamines were available far more cheaply than foreign cocaine, their effects lasted longer, and they could be taken by mouth.

In 1970, Congress passed the Controlled Substances Act, which helped reduce the supply of legally manufactured am-

Vice-President George Bush attends a drug-education class. Designer drugs are made in America; efforts to control their use must focus on reducing American demand rather than stamping out foreign supplies.

Los Angeles County sheriffs demonstrate a net that can be used to subdue people who become violent while under the influence of PCP.

phetamines by 80 percent. At this point, the importation and use of cocaine slowly began to rise again. The epidemic of cocaine and "crack" use we are experiencing today in America is partly a result of the shift away from amphetamines.

This seems to suggest that if the present efforts to reduce cocaine supply are successful, an increase in underground amphetamine production, or a search for a synthetic substitute for cocaine, could result.

How can this demand for substitutes be reduced? Education seems to be the likeliest answer to reducing the demand for cocaine substitutes. The more that people know about drugs — their history, actions, and side effects — the better they can arm themselves against their seductive lure.

The establishment of a national Cocaine Hotline (1-800-COCAINE) was a useful initial step, as are televised anti-drug commercials like the National Basketball Association's "Don't Foul Up" campaign. Growing media publicity, the development of drug-education and hospital rehabilitation programs for drug users, and the establishment of organizations such as Narcotics Anonymous (NA) and Cocaine Anonymous (CA) are also steps in the right direction.

Another important way to reduce the demand for illegal drugs is to explore drug-free alternatives that provide satisfaction equal to or greater than the feelings caused by drugs. In the next chapter we will discuss a few of the many options available.

Karate is a martial art that disciplines both the mind and body. It can improve flexibility and endurance, enhance spatial perception, raise self-confidence, and even reduce anger and frustration.

CHAPTER 8

DRUG-FREE
ALTERNATIVES

Humans may need to alter their consciousness from time to time. They have certainly looked for ways to do so since the dawn of time, with or without the help of psychoactive drugs. In cultures where drug use is integrated into society, it may strengthen social or religious ties between members in a positive way. For example, members of the Native American church use the organic psychoactive plant *peyote* in religious rituals to achieve altered states of consciousness that put them in touch with the Divine. There are no substance-abuse problems among members of this religious group. In fact, the Native American church has had great success in combating the alcoholism that victimizes many American Indians.

American society as a whole, however, does not promote communal drug use. In view of the negative side effects and the legal and social penalties for drug abuse in this country, alternatives are well worth exploring.

To be of value, these alternatives must offer pleasure, have long-term effects, and be able to compete successfully with drugs.

Unfortunately, nonchemical ways of changing consciousness generally produce less intense physical effects than drugs do. They require more active involvement by the user and more time, and their results are usually more subtle.

On the bright side, most alternatives to drug use are legal and generally produce positive, rather than negative, side effects. Because they require an active investment of time and energy, they shape our characters over the long run. Above all, mastering any of the following drug-free alternatives increases self-confidence, because they prove beyond doubt that we can alter our perception, thinking, or emotions without depending on chemicals outside ourselves.

Sports and Exercise

Sports and exercise change us physically over time — usually for the better — by increasing our heart and lung capacity, endurance or stamina, and muscle tone. These physical changes eventually have emotional consequences.

Running regularly increases endorphin levels in the brain, which results in heightened feelings of well-being. This type of vigorous aerobic exercise also helps regulate heartbeat and blood pressure.

Running regularly, for example, causes an increase in endorphin levels, with accompanying subjective feelings of calm and tranquility. Because endorphins tend to be released after stress reactions, the response to any situation or activity partly depends on how much energy is expended. With time, running reduces the heart rate and the blood pressure.

Sports are also a constructive way to work out stress and release aggressive feelings. Team sports, in particular, both help to release aggression and teach their players how to cooperate as a group.

Karate and T'ai Chi, both forms of martial arts, can be as beneficial as other forms of physical exercise. Furthermore, martial-arts training not only helps to develop the body, but also a set of mental attitudes that can last a lifetime. One man with a karate "brown belt," who had studied this martial art intensively for four years, listed the following changes in his life: He felt much more spontaneous, and his reflexes, both physical and mental, became more rapid. He feared pain less and his awareness of his environment was greater. His spatial perception changed so that he perceived not only objects, but the shape of the space around them. His self-confidence increased, and his level of anger was much lower.

T'ai Chi is a set of connected exercises that can be learned by young and old alike. The exercises are not taught for attack and defense, but more generally to improve balance and spatial perception. The benefits tend to include greater mental clarity and calm. Interestingly, T'ai Chi should be taught before any karate instruction, or after a student attains "black belt," but the two should not be taught simultaneously, because karate is oriented outward in space and is "aggressive," whereas T'ai Chi is oriented toward inner balance in space and is "passive." Purists feel that the two orientations should not be mixed.

Roads to Self-discovery

Physical activities that improve health have been highly publicized in the 1970s and 1980s. But non-drug alternatives do not necessarily involve physical activity. In fact, for some personalities the "inner journey" is more important.

Biofeedback and meditation both produce measurable changes in heart rate and blood pressure. Biofeedback training, in particular, is an intriguing modern concept, since it "teaches" us to voluntarily alter several body functions that have traditionally been considered involuntary or beyond our conscious control. These functions include the digestion rate and some brain-wave activity.

Daydreaming can also be beneficial. In an action-oriented society the stereotype of the "dreamer" is that of an odd, weak, or somehow defective person. But this is far from the truth.

It would be more accurate to describe daydreaming as an intellectual skill, part of the human arsenal of mental tools. Used as a form of "picture thinking," daydreaming helps us imagine many solutions to a problem — and the consequences of each solution—before deciding on what action to take.

Daydreaming is also an important preliminary activity to creative work, and can provide a mini-vacation from reality, with important effects similar to those of biofeedback or meditation.

Keeping a journal also increases self-knowledge. One benefit of keeping a journal is that it helps us to recognize our individual personality patterns. Each of us tends to do things, choose friends, and solve or create problems in a unique way. Particularly in adolescence, when change and growth are so rapid, a journal reminds us who we were and who we are becoming.

"Dream journals" became rather popular in the 1980s. Keeping a dream journal involves writing down dreams the minute one wakes up. Anyone willing to make this effort will begin to see patterns in dreams, just as in behavior. Over time, these patterns may tell us what we want, what we fear, what we love, and who we think we are.

Turning on Your "Inner Force"

Would you respond to an advertisement that listed three ways to travel through time and space — cheaply — with a guaranteed return? In fact, these forms of travel do exist — and have been available for thousands of years. They are art, music, and literature.

Human beings have recognized the powerful emotional appeal of music for thousands of years. Military music, for

A young woman follows a score while listening to classical music. Music has soothed and stimulated the human mind for millennia.

example, has a direct stimulant effect, including an increased heart and breathing rate. (It is no coincidence that most armies before World War II included drummers and fifers.) So do the national anthems of most countries, and specialized musical forms such as that played at bullfights.

One fundamental way in which music exerts its effects is by speeding up or slowing down the sense of time. Breathing and heart rates tend to synchronize themselves with musical time. Perhaps this pattern dates back to infancy, and our ability to fall asleep to the rhythm of a parent's heartbeat, a cradle's regular rocking, or the sound of a lullaby.

An example of music that slows the sense of time is Indian *sitar* music. This music slows one's rate of breathing, relaxes one's mood, and increases one's mental imagery. Over time, playing or listening to any type of music sensitizes us to musical patterns in the fabric of the everyday noises surrounding us.

A mother and her young daughter visit the "Harlem on My Mind" exhibit at New York City's Metropolitan Museum of Art. Both looking at and creating art can be relaxing and rewarding activities.

Singing and chanting increase carbon dioxide levels in the blood and lungs. In *Heaven and Hell*, a short book about visionary experience through the ages, the English author Aldous Huxley points out that after several hours, yoga breathing exercises, shouting, singing, and the chanting by monks of Christian or Buddhist texts all tend to increase the level of carbon dioxide in the body. The increase produces subtle perceptual changes, among them "swirls of patterned color" seen when the eyes are closed, and sudden recalls of past experiences.

The visual arts also transform vision. Try "climbing into" a painted landscape from another century, imagining the time of day, the weather, and the people you might encounter. Art explored for pleasure in this way is a form of "space travel," just as music is a form of "time travel." Humans can use both as healthy forms of temporary escape from reality, because to travel in this way we must make mental efforts that reward us with ever greater imaginative strength.

Creating art offers different benefits, including improved concentration, loss of the sense of time, and the ability to forget oneself. "Artistic" or not, try making a sketch of one of your hands. Look at the pores in the skin, the functional shapes of the fingers, the veins on the back of the hand. Any object you draw will never look the same to you again. This is because you have looked at it more closely than usual. With time, training yourself to view the world as an artist does will focus your visual memory enormously, and transform your entire visual world.

Literature is one of the most flexible art forms ever created. Almost everything can be translated into words: smells, feelings, sights, sounds, countries. The mind of the reader "retranslates" words into images. Making this translation effort strengthens us mentally. Obviously, though, books have meant far more over the centuries than just a set of strengthening exercises for humans. Books record human reactions to life, and so communicate with future generations. They give us role models, villains, imagined and real worlds — literally anything conceivable. What is not yet in a book may be there someday, imagined by men and women growing up now.

Students choose books at a local library. Literature is one of the most flexible art forms ever created, and allows the reader to transcend, however temporarily, the stresses of daily life.

A young boy and his dog. Studies have shown that relationships between pets and their owners are greatly beneficial for both partners.

Caring for Animals

Relationships between domestic pets and humans duplicate some elements of the child-parent relationship. They put the human being of any age in the position of a protective parent.

Studies done during the past decade have shown that this relationship benefits humans. Among elderly persons, for example, caring for a pet encourages physical activity, and may reduce depression. Prisoners who choose to care for animals as part of a rehabilitation program make more lasting progress (in terms of reduced levels of anger) than those without pets. Men and women of all ages tend to show a small decrease in blood pressure as they pet or talk to an animal. (Of course, this assumes that they have no physical allergies and do not fear or dislike the animal.)

In some ways, loving a pet is good training for loving other human beings and learning how to "connect" with them. And for most of us, learning to connect with other humans will remain our ultimate goal. No matter how valuable the love of animals may be, sooner or later most of us need to share these pleasures with other human beings.

Links with Other Humans

Of all the many ways to connect with others, religious and political groups offer one interesting advantage: they give us the power to change the world in cooperation with other men and women.

In the 19th century, the German political philospher Karl Marx condemned organized religions by describing them as "the opiate of the masses." Marx felt that poor people used religion as a narcotic to dull the pain of poverty and oppression. He felt that religion should be replaced by political organization.

Dr. Martin Luther King addresses a civil rights rally in 1964. This great leader demonstrated the strength of spiritual power, which he put to use in the fight against social injustice.

Two high school students at work in front of their school. By providing the satisfaction that comes from helping others, volunteer work benefits not only the community but the volunteer as well.

Religion itself, however, generates tremendous political power based on shared religious belief. The American black civil rights movement offers us a clear example of a positive use of religion in such a manner. The movement, led by the Reverend Martin Luther King, Jr., enabled a large number of black Americans to confront organized police violence in the South with nonviolence. This was in part a religious response suggested by Christian and Hindu philosophies.

Because members of churches or synagogues are cohesive groups with shared values, joining a religious group provides some of the same supports as belonging to a family.

Political and community groups offer similar benefits. The "inner force" of the human spirit may have difficulty growing in a destructive or hostile environment. This may explain why much, though not all, drug use is entwined with poverty in large cities. Drugs may provide the fastest escape from an intolerable reality. For those who believe that such outer factors as poverty shape our "inner" life, working for political or social change is a constructive choice.

If you are exploring ways to work for social change, you may want to start with volunteer programs in your community. These programs often welcome adolescents, because such programs are frequently underfunded and understaffed, and welcome injections of idealism and physical energy from young people.

Tutoring, staffing free lunch programs for the elderly or the sick, volunteering at the American Society for the Prevention of Cruelty to Animals (ASPCA), or joining a block association are all useful starting points for community activity. Your school may provide a list of local groups that actively recruit young people.

If you have already focused on issues that interest you (for example, military policy, human rights, animal rights, the environment), try calling the office of your local congressman or assemblyman. List your skills and the amount of time you have to volunteer, and ask where you fit in.

The few alternatives listed here are subjective choices based on personal values. As such, they barely scratch the surface of available choices. Not all alternatives appeal to all people, nor should they. Alternatives will change, overlap, and be discarded as you change and grow.

But one thing still remains clear — turning to chemicals for solace or escape is never without danger, and as in the case of designer drug deaths, can prove to be the end to all your problems—and your hopes.

APPENDIX

State Agencies
for the Prevention and Treatment
of Drug Abuse

ALABAMA
Department of Mental Health
Division of Mental Illness and
   Substance Abuse Community
   Programs
200 Interstate Park Drive
P.O. Box 3710
Montgomery, AL 36193
(205) 271-9253

ALASKA
Department of Health and Social
   Services
Office of Alcoholism and Drug
   Abuse
Pouch H-05-F
Juneau, AK 99811
(907) 586-6201

ARIZONA
Department of Health Services
Division of Behavioral Health
   Services
Bureau of Community Services
Alcohol Abuse and Alcoholism
   Section
2500 East Van Buren
Phoenix, AZ 85008
(602) 255-1238

Department of Health Services
Division of Behavioral Health
   Services
Bureau of Community Services
Drug Abuse Section
2500 East Van Buren
Phoenix, AZ 85008
( ) 255-1240

ARKANSAS
Department of Human Services
Office of Alcohol and Drug Abuse
   Prevention
1515 West 7th Avenue
Suite 310
Little Rock, AR 72202
(501) 371-2603

CALIFORNIA
Department of Alcohol and Drug
   Abuse
111 Capitol Mall
Sacramento, CA 95814
(916) 445-1940

COLORADO
Department of Health
Alcohol and Drug Abuse Division
4210 East 11th Avenue
Denver, CO 80220
(303) 320-6137

CONNECTICUT
Alcohol and Drug Abuse
   Commission
999 Asylum Avenue
3rd Floor
Hartford, CT 06105
(203) 566-4145

DELAWARE
Division of Mental Health
Bureau of Alcoholism and Drug
   Abuse
1901 North Dupont Highway
Newcastle, DE 19720
(302) 421-6101

DISTRICT OF COLUMBIA
Department of Human Services
Office of Health Planning and
    Development
601 Indiana Avenue, NW
Suite 500
Washington, D.C. 20004
(202) 724-5641

FLORIDA
Department of Health and
    Rehabilitative Services
Alcoholic Rehabilitation Program
1317 Winewood Boulevard
Room 187A
Tallahassee, FL 32301
(904) 488-0396

Department of Health and
    Rehabilitative Services
Drug Abuse Program
1317 Winewood Boulevard
Building 6, Room 155
Tallahassee, FL 32301
(904) 488-0900

GEORGIA
Department of Human Resources
Division of Mental Health and
    Mental Retardation
Alcohol and Drug Section
618 Ponce De Leon Avenue, NE
Atlanta, GA 30365-2101
(404) 894-4785

HAWAII
Department of Health
Mental Health Division
Alcohol and Drug Abuse Branch
1250 Punch Bowl Street
P.O. Box 3378
Honolulu, HI 96801
(808) 548-4280

IDAHO
Department of Health and Welfare
Bureau of Preventive Medicine
Substance Abuse Section
450 West State
Boise, ID 83720
(208) 334-4368

ILLINOIS
Department of Mental Health and
    Developmental Disabilities
Division of Alcoholism
160 North La Salle Street
Room 1500
Chicago, IL 60601
(312) 793-2907

Illinois Dangerous Drugs
    Commission
300 North State Street
Suite 1500
Chicago, IL 60610
(312) 822-9860

INDIANA
Department of Mental Health
Division of Addiction Services
429 North Pennsylvania Street
Indianapolis, IN 46204
(317) 232-7816

IOWA
Department of Substance Abuse
505 5th Avenue
Insurance Exchange Building
Suite 202
Des Moines, IA 50319
(515) 281-3641

KANSAS
Department of Social Rehabilitation
Alcohol and Drug Abuse Services
2700 West 6th Street
Biddle Building
Topeka, KS 66606
(913) 296-3925

KENTUCKY
Cabinet for Human Resources
Department of Health Services
Substance Abuse Branch
275 East Main Street
Frankfort, KY 40601
(502) 564-2880

LOUISIANA
Department of Health and Human
  Resources
Office of Mental Health and
  Substance Abuse
655 North 5th Street
P.O. Box 4049
Baton Rouge, LA 70821
(504) 342-2565

MAINE
Department of Human Services
Office of Alcoholism and Drug
  Abuse Prevention
Bureau of Rehabilitation
32 Winthrop Street
Augusta, ME 04330
(207) 289-2781

MARYLAND
Alcoholism Control Administration
201 West Preston Street
Fourth Floor
Baltimore, MD 21201
(301) 383-2977

State Health Department
Drug Abuse Administration
201 West Preston Street
Baltimore, MD 21201
(301) 383-3312

MASSACHUSETTS
Department of Public Health
Division of Alcoholism
755 Boylston Street
Sixth Floor
Boston, MA 02116
(617) 727-1960

Department of Public Health
Division of Drug Rehabilitation
600 Washington Street
Boston, MA 02114
(617) 727-8617

MICHIGAN
Department of Public Health
Office of Substance Abuse Services
3500 North Logan Street
P.O. Box 30035
Lansing, MI 48909
(517) 373-8603

MINNESOTA
Department of Public Welfare
Chemical Dependency Program
  Division
Centennial Building
658 Cedar Street
4th Floor
Saint Paul, MN 55155
(612) 296-4614

MISSISSIPPI
Department of Mental Health
Division of Alcohol and Drug Abuse
1102 Robert E. Lee Building
Jackson, MS 39201
(601) 359-1297

MISSOURI
Department of Mental Health
Division of Alcoholism and Drug
  Abuse
2002 Missouri Boulevard
P.O. Box 687
Jefferson City, MO 65102
(314) 751-4942

MONTANA
Department of Institutions
Alcohol and Drug Abuse Division
1539 11th Avenue
Helena, MT 59620
(406) 449-2827

NEBRASKA
Department of Public Institutions
Division of Alcoholism and Drug
Abuse
801 West Van Dorn Street
P.O. Box 94728
Lincoln, NB 68509
(402) 471-2851, Ext. 415

NEVADA
Department of Human Resources
Bureau of Alcohol and Drug Abuse
505 East King Street
Carson City, NV 89710
(702) 885-4790

NEW HAMPSHIRE
Department of Health and Welfare
Office of Alcohol and Drug Abuse
   Prevention
Hazen Drive
Health and Welfare Building
Concord, NH 03301
(603) 271-4627

NEW JERSEY
Department of Health
Division of Alcoholism
129 East Hanover Street CN 362
Trenton, NJ 08625
(609) 292-8949

Department of Health
Division of Narcotic and Drug
   Abuse Control
129 East Hanover Street CN 362
Trenton, NJ 08625
(609) 292-8949

NEW MEXICO
Health and Environment Department
Behavioral Services Division
Substance Abuse Bureau
725 Saint Michaels Drive
P.O. Box 968
Santa Fe, NM 87503
(505) 984-0020, Ext. 304

NEW YORK
Division of Alcoholism and Alcohol
   Abuse
194 Washington Avenue
Albany, NY 12210
(518) 474-5417

Division of Substance Abuse
   Services
Executive Park South
Box 8200
Albany, NY 12203
(518) 457-7629

NORTH CAROLINA
Department of Human Resources
Division of Mental Health, Mental
   Retardation and Substance Abuse
   Services
Alcohol and Drug Abuse Services
325 North Salisbury Street
Albemarle Building
Raleigh, NC 27611
(919) 733-4670

NORTH DAKOTA
Department of Human Services
Division of Alcoholism and Drug
   Abuse
State Capitol Building
Bismarck, ND 58505
(701) 224-2767

OHIO
Department of Health
Division of Alcoholism
246 North High Street
P.O. Box 118
Columbus, OH 43216
(614) 466-3543

Department of Mental Health
Bureau of Drug Abuse
65 South Front Street
Columbus, OH 43215
(614) 466-9023

OKLAHOMA
Department of Mental Health
Alcohol and Drug Programs
4545 North Lincoln Boulevard
Suite 100 East Terrace
P.O. Box 53277
Oklahoma City, OK 73152
(405) 521-0044

OREGON
Department of Human Resources
Mental Health Division
Office of Programs for Alcohol and
  Drug Problems
2575 Bittern Street, NE
Salem, OR 97310
(503) 378-2163

PENNSYLVANIA
Department of Health
Office of Drug and Alcohol
  Programs
Commonwealth and Forster Avenues
Health and Welfare Building
P.O. Box 90
Harrisburg, PA 17108
(717) 787-9857

RHODE ISLAND
Department of Mental Health,
  Mental Retardation and Hospitals
Division of Substance Abuse
Substance Abuse Administration
  Building
Cranston, RI 02920
(401) 464-2091

SOUTH CAROLINA
Commission on Alcohol and Drug
  Abuse
3700 Forest Drive
Columbia, SC 29204
(803) 758-2521

SOUTH DAKOTA
Department of Health
Division of Alcohol and Drug Abuse
523 East Capitol, Joe Foss Building
Pierre, SD 57501
(605) 773-4806

TENNESSEE
Department of Mental Health and
  Mental Retardation
Alcohol and Drug Abuse Services
505 Deaderick Street
James K. Polk Building,
  Fourth Floor
Nashville, TN 37219
(615) 741-1921

TEXAS
Commission on Alcoholism
809 Sam Houston State Office
  Building
Austin, TX 78701
(512) 475-2577
Department of Community Affairs
Drug Abuse Prevention Division
2015 South Interstate Highway 35
P.O. Box 13166
Austin, TX 78711
(512) 443-4100

UTAH
Department of Social Services
Division of Alcoholism and Drugs
150 West North Temple
Suite 350
P.O. Box 2500
Salt Lake City, UT 84110
(801) 533-6532

VERMONT
Agency of Human Services
Department of Social and
  Rehabilitation Services
Alcohol and Drug Abuse Division
103 South Main Street
Waterbury, VT 05676
(802) 241-2170

VIRGINIA
Department of Mental Health and
  Mental Retardation
Division of Substance Abuse
109 Governor Street
P.O. Box 1797
Richmond, VA 23214
(804) 786-5313

WASHINGTON
Department of Social and Health
  Service
Bureau of Alcohol and Substance
  Abuse
Office Building—44 W
Olympia, WA 98504
(206) 753-5866

WEST VIRGINIA
Department of Health
Office of Behavioral Health Services
Division on Alcoholism and Drug
  Abuse
1800 Washington Street East
Building 3 Room 451
Charleston, WV 25305
(304) 348-2276

WISCONSIN
Department of Health and Social
  Services
Division of Community Services
Bureau of Community Programs
Alcohol and Other Drug Abuse
  Program Office
1 West Wilson Street
P.O. Box 7851
Madison, WI 53707
(608) 266-2717

WYOMING
Alcohol and Drug Abuse Programs
Hathaway Building
Cheyenne, WY 82002
(307) 777-7115, Ext. 7118

GUAM
Mental Health & Substance Abuse
  Agency
P.O. Box 20999
Guam 96921

PUERTO RICO
Department of Addiction Control
  Services
Alcohol Abuse Programs
P.O. Box B-Y Rio Piedras Station
Rio Piedras, PR 00928
(809) 763-5014

Department of Addiction Control
  Services
Drug Abuse Programs
P.O. Box B-Y Rio Piedras Station
Rio Piedras, PR 00928
(809) 764-8140

VIRGIN ISLANDS
Division of Mental Health,
  Alcoholism & Drug Dependency
  Services
P.O. Box 7329
Saint Thomas, Virgin Islands 00801
(809) 774-7265

AMERICAN SAMOA
LBJ Tropical Medical Center
Department of Mental Health Clinic
Pago Pago, American Samoa 96799

TRUST TERRITORIES
Director of Health Services
Office of the High Commissioner
Saipan, Trust Territories 96950

Further Reading

Brecher, Edward M. *Licit and Illicit Drugs*. Boston: Little, Brown, 1972.

Kirsch, M. M. *Designer Drugs*. Minneapolis, MN: Comp-Care, 1986.

LeShan, Lawrence. *How to Meditate*. New York: Bantam, 1975.

Macdonald, Ian Donald, M.D. "Drug Abuse in Adolescents," in *Post-graduate Medicine 78,* Minneapolis, MN: McGraw-Hill, Vol. 4, pp. 109-113: September 15, 1985.

Rosen, Winifred, and Andrew Weil, M.D. *Chocolate to Morphine*. Boston: Houghton Mifflin, 1983.

Shafer, Jack. "Designer Drugs," in *Science 85*, Washington, D.C.: American Association for the Advancement of Science, pp. 60-66: March, 1985.

Glossary

addiction a condition caused by repeated drug use, characterized by a compulsive urge to continue using the drug, a tendency to increase the dosage, and physiological and/or psychological dependence

adulterate to add an extra ingredient to a pure substance, increasing the quantity but decreasing the quality of that substance

amphetamine a drug that stimulates the central nervous system, alleviates fatigue, and produces a feeling of alertness and well-being. Although it has been used for weight control, repeated use of the drug can cause restlessness and insomnia.

analog a chemical compound whose chemical nucleus resembles that of another compound and produces similar effects

biochemical a chemical produced by living things to help them perform the vital functions; examples include enzymes and neurotransmitters

central nervous system the brain and the spinal cord

cocaine the primary psychoactive ingredient in the coca plant; it functions as a behavioral stimulant

coma deep unconsciousness that may last for hours, days, or even years

crack a crude, relatively inexpensive, highly addictive form of cocaine

demerol an opiate used to relieve pain; highly addictive

derivative a drug produced from another substance. Morphine is derived from opium.

designer drug a synthetic drug produced by chemically altering the structure of the original, often illicit, drug; a drug that has been redesigned to increase appeal. Crack is a redesigned form of cocaine.

diagnosis use of tests, observation, and medical history to discover what condition or disease a person has

dopamine an important neurotransmitter in the brain concerned with motor function and emotional response

endogenous made within a cell or organism

endorphins compounds produced in the brain that serve as the body's natural opiates

fentanyl a synthetic drug with effects similar to those of morphine, but more potent

hallucinogen a drug that produces sensory impressions that have no basis in reality

heroin a semisynthetic opiate produced from a chemical modification of morphine

LSD (lysergic acid diethylamide) a hallucinogenic drug derived from fungus that grows on rye or from morning-glory seeds

morphine an addictive drug derived from opium and used as a sedative or anesthetic

narcotic originally a group of drugs producing effects similar to those of morphine; often used to refer to any substance that sedates, has a depressive effect, and/or causes dependence

neurotoxin any substance poisonous to any part of a nerve cell

neurotransmitter a biochemical that helps to transmit signals from one nerve to another in the brain and central nervous system

opiate any compound from the milky juice of the poppy plant, *Papaver somniferum*, including opium, morphine, codeine, and heroin

paranoid schizophrenia a psychiatric disorder characterized by extreme suspicion and an altered view of reality

Parkinson's disease a disease of the central nervous system causing tremor and muscular weakness or paralysis; found predominantly among elderly people

physical dependence an adaptation of the body to the presence of a drug such that its absence produces withdrawal symptoms

psychedelic producing hallucinations or having mind-altering properties

psychological dependence a condition in which the drug user craves a drug to maintain a sense of well-being and feels discomfort when deprived of it

psychosis a mental disease characterized by hallucinations, mood disturbances, and loss of contact with reality

receptors specialized areas on the nerve cells adapted to receive neurotransmitters

synapse the space between adjoining nerve cells in a nerve pathway

synthesize to combine chemicals to create a new substance

tolerance a decrease of susceptibility to the effects of a drug due to its continued administration, resulting in the user's need to increase the drug dosage in order to achieve the effects experienced previously

withdrawal the physiological and psychological effects of discontinued use of a drug

PICTURE CREDITS

Index

Paula Goodman spent several years working as a medical copywriter for a pharmaceutical advertising agency. Subsequently she began to free-lance as a writer with a special interest in health and nutrition. She combines free-lance writing with free-lance illustration "in order to exercise both sides of [her] brain."

Gabriel Koz, M.D., is a psychiatrist with a special interest in the problems of inner-city residents. He is chief of psychiatry at Woodhull, a city hospital in Brooklyn, New York. He is also chief of psychiatry at New York University. He arrived in the United States in 1962, on a Fulbright Fellowship to Harvard, after completing his training at a small psychiatric teaching hospital in London.

Solomon H. Snyder, M.D., is Distinguished Service Professor of Neuroscience, Pharmacology and Psychiatry at The Johns Hopkins University School of Medicine. He has served as president of the Society for Neuroscience and in 1978 received the Albert Lasker Award in Medical Research. He has authored *Uses of Marijuana, Madness and the Brain, The Troubled Mind, Biological Aspects of Mental Disorder,* and edited *Perspective in Neuropharmacology: A Tribute to Julius Axelrod.* Professor Snyder was a research associate with Dr. Axelrod at the National Institutes of Health.

Barry L. Jacobs, Ph.D., is currently a professor in the program of neuroscience at Princeton University. Professor Jacobs is author of *Serotonin Neurotransmission and Behavior* and *Hallucinogens: Neurochemical, Behavioral and Clinical Perspectives.* He has written many journal articles in the field of neuroscience and contributed numerous chapters to books on behavior and brain science. He has been a member of several panels of the National Institute of Mental Health.

Joann Ellison Rodgers, M.S. (Columbia), became Deputy Director of Public Affairs and Director of Media Relations for the Johns Hopkins Medical Institutions in Baltimore, Maryland, in 1984 after 18 years as an award-winning science journalist and widely read columnist for the Hearst newspapers.